Journey on the Kingdom Road

Bud Surles, D. Min.

Dedication

I dedicate this book to my Ziggy.
She is the love of my life, the strength of my feet, and the
joyous gift of God that makes me whole.

Foreword

❖

Community transformation has become a red-hot topic in Western Christendom with scores of advocates and coaches brandishing their own special recipes for success. Unfortunately, actual results continue to go unrealized in most communities.

A big reason for this failure is the mistaken belief that corporate revival begins with collective action. Unlike the fabled Boston Marathon, the journey to transformation does not begin with hordes of people crowding the starting line. Whether we like it or not, God's rules for this event require that we run the first stages in isolation. In other words, community transformation must of necessity be preceded by personal transformation.

Individual change is the part of our journey that most of us would just as soon skip — and, sadly, many do. This neglect is not so much born out of ignorance as it is a lack of appetite. Notwithstanding our rhetoric to the contrary, we are simply not that hungry for God's presence and ways.

Bud Surles' Journey on the Kingdom Road offers a powerful stimulant to this diminished appetite. Refreshingly free of pretense and cliché, this book takes readers to the heart of the matter — to relationship. This is crucial, because if we fail to appreciate the essence of our journey, we will certainly fail to reach our destination.

I truly enjoyed this book, and I believe you will too. Bud Surles is a man of the land, and his illustrations drawn from the wide open spaces of the American West show that he is also a keen observer. Have you ever wondered what it is like to bite a porcupine? Read on. Do you want to gaze on the incomparable beauty of the Cold Spring area of Wyoming? The secrets are here.

Make no mistake however. The illustrations in this book pack a punch. Journey on the Kingdom Road is intended for your night stand, not your coffee table. So get out your yellow highlighter and savor the practical insights that Bud Surles has assembled between the covers of this outstanding book.

George Otis, Jr.
Lynnwood, Washington

Endorsements

✦

" "Bud's book is very conversational and engaging . . . His
great strength is in the stories he tells, his own parables. I
loved the story about the family mailbox, a wonderful illustration. My favorite story, though, was of the Irish Setter
— poignant and perfectly illustrates the consequences of
unforgiveness. Bud's book will help every reader travel
farther down the Kingdom Road."

—*Cher Smith, theculturebeat.com*

"As followers of Christ walk the Kingdom Road, we best be
going the right direction, for the right reason. Bud's writing
helps us keep our eye on the goal, and make the most of the
journey along the way. This book is true to Scripture, offers
fresh insight, and speaks to real life. Written with a style of
a good friend sharing his heart, this book will touch yours.
Helpful indeed!"

—Stan Hankins – International Evangelist for *Ambassadors*
for Christ

"Feel frustrated with life's spin-outs and breakdowns? Here
are tested text messages that will get you on the road again

and headed in the right direction. JOURNEY ON THE KINGDOM ROAD is a scenic, five star Trip-Tic to God's kingdom. Buckle up, gear down for Dr. Bud's Triple A insights."

—Rev. Dr. John Gilmore, Over-seas Lecturer, Spurgeon's School of Theology and Author of Probing Heaven, *Too Young To Be Old, Ambushed Åt Sunset, The Trials of Christ, Lotto—Fun or Folly?, Pastoral Politics*, and *Sure Enough—9 Views of Salvation-Assurance.*

Table of Contents

Acknowledgements

ༀ

I have many friends I discourse with daily. Without their help I could not write a word. And if you have not met my friends, I invite you to join with me in our daily meetings. Let me introduce you to them, for without them there would be no journey on the Kingdom Road for me. First of all, I want to introduce you to International Evangelist, Stan Hankins. He is my best friend, outside of my wife. He is my confidant, my mentor, and the instrument God used to call me into the ministry.

But there are other friends – best friends, people I have never met. J. I. Packer, R. C. Sproul, Dallas Willard, John Piper, Richard Foster, George Otis, Jr., Bill Hull, and John Stott are my living friends. Out of their powerful relationships with God, I learn a little more each day. The problem is, their thoughts and ideas have become so entrenched in my own thinking, I hardly know when I am speaking from their words or my own. So I beg understanding and forgiveness when their ideas are repeated without proper notations.

Besides my living friends I want to pay tribute to friends who mean so much to me who are now with the Lord. James Montgomery Boice, Oswald Chambers, Dietrich Bonhoeffer, Alexander Campbell, John Wesley, Philip Spener, George Mueller, Martin Luther, St. Augustine, and most importantly the Apostle Paul. How I love walking with them in our mutual journeys to God.

I want to give thanks and tribute to these men of God who shape my thoughts and helped me grow in my Lord.

Introduction

*Christianity is a gateway into God. And then when you get
into God, with Christ in God, then you're on a journey into
infinity, into infinitude. – A. W. Tozer[1]*

*This is what the Lord says: "Stand at the crossroads and
look; ask for the ancient paths, ask where the good way is,
and walk in it, and you will find rest for your souls."
(Jer. 6:16)*

Life is a journey. From conception in our mother's
womb until we take our last breath on this earth, we are
pilgrims and sojourners en route to our eternal destiny. For
some, the journey ends in the womb, for others, tragedy cuts
the life short of its potential years. For many, life's journey
progresses until the body can no longer contain the spirit
within. But in all cases, life is a journey.

During the course of our journey we are ruled by many
kings – some major and some minor. But there is one king
at the beginning of every human life who is supreme. That
king is self. No earthly king can overrule the king of self.
The parent kings can tell a child what to do, but the decision
of whether or not he or she will do it is up to the child. An
employer king can tell an employee what to do, but the king

of self makes the decision of what to follow. The government king can make many laws directing behavior, but the king of self is supreme even over the government king. No earthly king can make the self-king make right decisions. Left alone, the self-king is bent on misery – both now and forever.

But there is a King, who can enter a human life and take control. He can rule over the self-king in such a way that the individual's life journey has meaning, joy, purpose, power, and effectiveness. Once the self-king surrenders its authority to Jesus Christ – the God King – the individual journey is on a new road. Let me call it the Kingdom Road.

This book is all about a journey on that road. What does the journey look like? Indeed, what does the road look like? And why should the king of me surrender to the King of the Universe? Why should I give up my rights to myself to follow a King who was crucified 2,000 years ago? This book will attempt to answer those questions, not with my words, but with the words of the King Himself.

I believe that Jesus Christ is the most compelling figure in all of human history. He came preaching the Kingdom of God. And there is something about that Kingdom that is Good News. What is the Good News? Is it pie in the sky that we obtain by some sort of religious conviction, dogma, or commitment? Is it a moral rule for life, which demonstrates how to have an orderly society? Yes, most certainly it is those things. However, conviction, dogma, commitment, and moral order are only microscopic elements of what Jesus came to demonstrate. The real Good News of the King and His Kingdom is that they are readily available. Salvation is not some futuristic event. It is a powerful, life-changing phenomenon that occurs upon surrender of the self-king to Jesus Christ. When that happens the human tragedy caused by following other roads is exploded, and bright new eternal life begins – Today.

In one sense the Kingdom of God is futuristic. Jesus will return and establish His eternal righteous rule and reign. And when He does, heartache, illness, mistreatment, and cruelty will all come to an immediate end (Matt. 25:34; 1 Cor. 15:34) for those who are in Christ Jesus. The Kingdom is also futuristic in the sense that believers will immediately upon expiration of their bodies be with Christ in the visible Kingdom (Matt. 26:29). However, the Kingdom is also near, at hand, within grasp (Mk. 1:15, etc.). The Kingdom of God is a short step away and is available now. Jesus wanted us to know that. And acquiring that Kingdom lies within the grasp of every individual. That is Good News. The acquisition begins with a heart commitment to the King. You see, the heart is the final place where the Kingdom can be found. Jesus said the Kingdom of God is within us (Lk. 17:21).

A kingdom, any kingdom, is where a king reigns. A king is the moral, righteous, ethical, and legal ruler and authority under which that kingdom is governed. So when Christ comes again, He will rule in righteousness. There will be no alternatives. But He can rule even today. That is Good News. He can take over an individual life, and then one life at a time begin to penetrate the culture, and the Kingdom of God will come shining through as a brilliant light in a dark and foreboding world.

So what does the Kingdom of God look like? Why is it good news? What should compel me to take the journey on the Kingdom Road? Since that is the subject of the book, I will not attempt a complete answer here, but we need to see enough of the answer to urge us to walk farther, dig deeper, and see if the journey is worthy of our time.

The Kingdom of God looks like a place where the citizens love God with all their hearts, souls, minds, and strength; they love one another as Christ loved them; and every citizen is compelled by that love to share their King and His Good News with others. The best place to find out about such a

Kingdom is to understand the greatest Kingdom Message ever delivered. The Message was delivered by the King Himself, and its purpose, I will defend, is to demonstrate that in no other kingdom does life have purpose, meaning, power, and effectiveness (Rom. 14:17; 1 Cor. 4:20). The Message states that in no other kingdom can we find peace and joy in the present and guarantees for the future; in no other kingdom are we allowed to walk daily with our King. That Message has been called historically the Sermon on the Mount.

From this point forward, however, I will refer to this sermon as the Sermon on the Kingdom Road. In this Sermon, the King lays out a pathway for individuals, the Church, and the culture to find the joy, inner peace, and resplendent obedience that makes sense (Heb. 10:28). The road has a map. The map is what we have come to know as the Beatitudes. Then comes a description of the journey, when Jesus describes the Kingdom Road as a road built upon the condition of the heart. A heart condition shapes what a person looks like, and the heart shaped by God reflects His image. Therefore, the King describes Kingdom people. And finally the King lays before His hearers and readers the reality of choice – two gates, two pathways, two builders. From Adam and Eve to the present there is always that pesky thing called choice – God's way or the way that leads to destruction. The Sermon on the Kingdom Road provides a divine connection between the life of Christ and a life that leads to everything we want in this life and the next. It is a connection between the King and His followers.

Life is a journey for every human being. There are many choices of roads. But for everyone, there is a King who is calling us to make that journey on the Kingdom Road. It is not an easy road. In fact the King calls it narrow. But it is a wonderful road, for on it and it alone, we will find rest for our souls, peace in our hearts, the purpose for which we were created, and we will walk daily, for eternity, with our King.

So join me in this fascinating journey on the Kingdom Road. We will begin where every well thought out journey begins. We will start with a map, a vision of what the journey will be like. Church history has called this map the Beatitudes. Once the journey is launched, we will go down the Kingdom Road. Its pavement is gold, but not the glittery stuff. It is a gold that emerges from the heart. On any journey there are gas stations, cafes, and rest stops to get renewed, to stretch your legs, and to splash water on your face. The rest stop on this journey is the Lord's Prayer. And then comes the final destination. It is a Kingdom, a state of mind that is focused, worry free, and filled with all the right choices. And when we arrive, we will find that our course has been deliberate, our journey refreshing, and that our foundations are rock solid.

Chapter 1

Connecting the Dots

❦

Now when He saw the crowds, Jesus went up on a
mountainside and sat down. His disciples came to Him,
and He began to teach them . . ." (Matt. 5:1)

If the axiom "A journey of a thousand miles begins with
a single step," as laid down by Confucius is true, (and I
am not troubled when even a pagan speaks truth), then, like
all journeys, the journey on the Kingdom Road must begin
with a single step. The reason to take that step, I challenge,
is that *there is a compelling reason to take the journey.* If life
is rapidly passing you by, if tragedy has gripped your heart
and existence does not make sense, if burdens overwhelm
you, or if life generally has become "so daily," those things
may be compelling reason enough. But those are negative
reasons. You do not have to be in the pits of life to see that
there must be a more excellent way, a brighter path, and
more meaningful purpose for this life. So whether you are
troubled by life or simply want to attain the very best that
God has in store for you, you will find the Kingdom Road
a very compelling journey. And the King is sitting down,
asking you (His disciples) to come and He will teach you.

Before we begin any journey, however, we must have confidence the Road leads to somewhere, or to some thing, that has significance for our lives. Thus, there are certain beliefs that we should embrace before this journey will make any sense. But even if you cannot fully embrace these beliefs now, I challenge you to at least be open to the possibility they are true. Let me outline those beliefs.

We must believe there is a connection between where we are now and the destination objective.

We must believe there is a connection between being a Christian and life in the trenches of the world.

We must believe there is a King who has earned the right to the Ultimate Title, which every word that comes from His mouth is truth, and that truth has profound meaning for life.

We must believe that He has answers to life's most perplexing questions that are far more effective than those given by pop media and philosophical gurus.

We must believe the reality that life in the Kingdom is truly the good life, and that all other life is a cheap substitute.

But I am getting ahead of myself. Maybe I have jumped all the way to the end. Because you see, Jesus began His ministry, not laying down un-achievable laws to obey, but rather by providing for us a way to meaning, purpose, power, and effectiveness in life. There is a connection between real life and Kingdom life. It is no accident that the King began His ministry by demonstrating this awesome connection. That is the purpose of the Message, the *Journey on the Kingdom Road.*

The Connection

I'll never forget when Daddy brought me that very special gift. It was a book, similar to a coloring book, but it was even greater. Each page contained numbers jumbled on the paper with only a few random lines. The more elementary pages had an arrow pointing to the number one, but as you got farther into the book, such helpful hints went away. Daddy was so proud when I could find the number one without help. The trick was to draw a line between one and two, two and three, three and four and so on until all the dots were connected. And as my little hands moved the soft leaded pencil from dot to dot, the image would come to life. My little creative juices flowed. There were over 100 puzzles in the "connect-the-dots" book. Truly it was one of my most treasured gifts.

The unbridled fascinations of childhood, however, become tainted by the realities of life. And just maybe that book warped my sense of reality. Maybe I began to look at life differently – that each dot was related to the other in some divine way that would produce what God wanted for our lives. Certainly, then, the teachings of Jesus must have had some other purpose in His inaugural sermon than to point to His character. Surely there was a purpose beyond giving His disciples some unattainable moral and ethical premise upon which they should live. Surely life on this earth had purpose and meaning or God would not have gone through the trouble of creating us.

I believe that most pastors see a connection between what Jesus taught and life on the Kingdom Road as they commit their lives to the Gospel. "The dots must somehow be connected," they reason. I know I did. But maybe I was a little too naive. When I began my ministry, I actually believed that each Christian was yearning to find that connection. That naivete, when confronted with modern reality, is what sends most ministers into burnout and other professions. Take Jack for example.

Jack was the most highly recruited senior in the seminary's history. He had everything a church wanted in a pastor – charisma, good looks, a preacher's voice, a firm grip on the gospel, and a beautiful bride-to-be that a congregation could dote on. Jack saw the divine connection of the King and His teachings and life to be lived on earth. He was in love with His King and was sure the Church was too. Already, via seminary sermons and pulpit supply, his reputation had spread from one end of the denomination to the other. All of this notoriety, deep down inside, irked Jack a little.

The seminary saw something unique in Jack far beyond his ability to preach and draw people to his message. They saw a gifted grasp of Scripture. He not only knew God's word, but seemed to be able to discern its meaning far beyond most seminarians. And Jack lived the Word. He had a dedication, not to Scripture, but to the One to whom all Scripture points. Jesus Christ was his very reason for being. When those elements in life are combined, a love for people ensues and there comes a powerful presentation of the gospel reserved for the most revered of Christianity.

The president of the seminary took a special interest in Jack. After all, any graduate would always be a reflection of the school from which he or she graduated. It was important, then, that the most influential in the denomination know about Jack. Every opportunity the president had to speak to a church leader about Jack, he spoke proudly and convincingly. Every major church within the denomination, whose pulpits or senior associate positions were vacant, received a call from the proud president. It was not surprising then, that by the end of his seminary education, Jack was so highly recruited.

The denomination wanted Jack in a staff position, to reach out to the churches that seemed to have lost their moorings. Non-affiliated groups wanted to use Jack in evangelism efforts. Para-church organizations wanted Jack to carry the banner for their causes. And of course there were the churches. Large churches, which normally required years of experience for a pastor, were openly recruiting Jack to come and fill their pulpits. One church, in particular, was of great interest to the seminary president. It was a wealthy church in a major southwestern city. It was a church that, with the right leadership, could be destined for national prominence. It could become a showcase. It had just the right location. The people who made up its membership were not only influential in the community, state, and nation, but they also *professed* sound theology. The combination was so right that evangelical Christianity could make large advances through this church with just the right leadership, and the seminary president believed that Jack was the right leader. The church overcame arguments of youth and inexperience by pointing to great pastors who ministered in a single church from seminary to retirement. In the end, everyone agreed, Jack was the man.

After graduation, Jack and his new bride were eagerly off to the sands of the Southwest. Like every seminary graduate, he was eager to preach the Good News. And like most ministries, Jack was given a gracious welcome and a beautiful — although short — honeymoon. (A church honeymoon is a period when the congregation presents its best foot forward to the new pastor. He is not exposed to the problems of the community, the inner politics of the church, nor the skeletons that lurk in the closets of the members.) It was during this time that Jack got to know the families. He prayed for them when they were sick, and he was there for them in their times of loss and need. It was a time of bonding and trust building. The church began to shine brightly in the denominational crown. The pews were full on Sunday mornings. There was a deep pride beginning to settle into the church. The seminary's most highly recruited student was their pastor. Combining this ecclesiastical honeymoon with a marital honeymoon, life was ecstatic for Jack. They were the happiest days of his young life.

But the honeymoon was short lived. After only a few months, Jack began to see the deep schisms that lay beneath the surface of the church and the community. The idealism of believing that God was making a difference in the life of people began to be shattered by a prominent member's affair. The State Senator, who was the Board's most powerful member, was under investigation for accepting bribes. Racial tensions, both in the community and in the church, became apparent. Divorces seemed to be part of the casual life of the congregation. Many nights were spent visiting youth from wealthy homes in jail for drug and alcohol- related crimes. And the church was having little impact on the community. There seemed to be an obvious disconnect between the gospel and life. Bars and stadiums were fuller than churches. Graft, corruption, licentious behavior, and greed, although just beneath the surface of respectability, became readily visible. All of this became a force that ejected Jack from the bliss of the honeymoon and catapulted him to the reality of Christian ministry.

The first hint of the racial prejudice in his own congregation came in a presentation to the board six months after his arrival. Jack was uncomfortable with the nearly all white mix of the church. While most of the community's minority population was Catholic, Jack was concerned about the unchurched of that group. Alcoholism was high. Family decadence was causing a dearth of unwed mothers, single parent and even no parent homes. Housing conditions were the worst he had seen in his young life. Poverty had robbed many of any hope for the future, and despair was everywhere among this group.

Jack felt a Kingdom- minded church must address the situation. He made a proposal to the board that proposed education of members, an extensive evangelism effort, and a helping- hand ministry effort to reach the unchurched in the minority community. The normally congenial board sat in a stunned silence as Jack joyously made his proposal. While no one wanted to be the voice of racism, the bigoted air became so thick, Jack could hardly breathe. The proposal was tabled while the board "took time to review the components." A committee was formed to study Jack's proposal in depth. And to head the committee, the most influential businessman in the area was appointed.

After a few weeks it was apparent that Jack's relationship with the board and even most of the congregation had dramatically changed. People were cordial enough, but coldness pervaded the atmosphere. Dinner invitations, which once filled the young couple's calendar, stopped entirely. His sermons, which early on, were always given lavish praise, now received no comment at all. Obvious foot dragging on the proposal was evident. Meeting after meeting the proposal was tabled to give the committee "more time" for an in-depth study.

It did not take the brightest and best of the seminary to recognize such stone-walling. Jack was heart-broken. The disconnect between the gospel and life in his congregation began to rip at his faith and self- assurance. It became clear: the people did not want to hear the true gospel of Jesus Christ. They only wanted sermons that made them feel good about themselves, to affirm lifestyles they (not their faith) had embraced. Certainly, there was no interest in a gospel that would penetrate their hearts. After much prayer Jack's real mission became clear. Prior to this moment, he saw his mission to attract people to the church, to preach the Good News to the lost, and to help the congregation see the importance of local and world mission. But the stark reality of a church that did not see the connection between the teachings of Christ and life on this earth imposed a new vision on Jack.

Now he was driven by the desire that his people know Jesus Christ. He wanted them to see that Christ was not only the most compelling figure in history, but that He could become equally compelling in our time and in our hearts. The connection between modern life and Christ's ministry, His death, and His resurrection had to be made visible, pertinent, and compelling to the people. The moment of that realization took this young minister from the shelter of a honeymoon, into the greatest adventure of his life. He began this adventure by teaching, preaching, and living the Sermon on the Kingdom Road.

Jack's desire was to demonstrate to people who called themselves "Christian" that there is a higher purpose in life – higher than the kings of earth proclaim – found only in the King and in His Kingdom. There is a connection between healthy marriage and His teachings. There is a viable link between His message and wise and ethical business practices. Vibrant human relationships are available, peace on earth is attainable, and anxiety and worry can be defeated. To do this he had to address the issues of pride, discipline, and money. He had to speak of serving God, and treating people with dignity. And his deepest desire was to do so in such a manner that the congregation would see the overwhelming evidence of the gospel's power of life and power over death. He wanted them to understand what Paul knew when he wrote, ". . . I am not ashamed of the gospel, for it is the power of God unto salvation for everyone who believes. . ." (Romans 1:16). Jack wanted his church to understand that real life as God intended it to be begins on the eternal journey. And the only road for which the journey is eternal is the Kingdom Road.

There is really no difference in the ministry of Jack and the ministry of the Lord he serves. Early in Jesus' ministry, He was very popular. He walked the region of Galilee, and His following grew as He healed the sick, gave sight to the blind, and began to preach the good news of the Kingdom. He, too, had a honeymoon. The people were the lost sheep of Israel, the politically oppressed, the slaves and the outcasts. And these people loved the message of Jesus – at least the message of healing, forgiveness of sins, and heaven.

We are like that. We love the Jesus who heals. We love to hear messages that address our needs, but require nothing from us in return. People flock to churches all over our land today, churches that totally focus on the good feelings of faith. We love it that God loves us, but we cringe when the gospel places demands upon our lives.

Jack's story has no ending. It is the story of transformation of hearts and lives, which is the continuing story of Christ on earth. It is the story of making the connection, one soul, one mission, one broken relationship at a time. The enduring story of Christ and Him crucified has the power to make that connection, and Jack's ministry, my ministry, all ministries can make a difference, because our King came to give humanity the Good News, that life can have meaning.

"Meaningless, meaningless," wrote the wealthy teacher. All life is meaningless, a chasing after the wind. The meaninglessness of Solomon's life was an Old Testament reality that can be remedied today by the New Testament proclamation of the Kingdom Road. However, we must acknowledge that the message of the gospel is a double- edged sword, dividing even the joints and the marrow, and eventually, hearers of its words. Every person must either begin the journey down the Road, or take another road. The gospel leaves no other choices. According to the King's own words, His road is narrow and few shall walk upon it.

Jesus was never content for miracles to be the totality of His message. While He knew that healing and stories of God's love might bring tranquility for a little while, He also knew it would do nothing to change the hearts of people. He knew that for the children of God to experience real life, both on earth and eternally, they must make the connection between the message of God and behavior. They had to accept that God's ways were higher than their own – that in the Kingdom, black must become white, pride must become humility, weapons of warfare must be love, fuel for the soul must be more important than fuel for the body, and that God must be the very priority of our lives. So Jesus took a small group of His followers to a mountaintop to teach them the deeper things of God.

Much has been said about this message and why Jesus preached it. Because it goes against the grain of world (and even modern Christian) opinion, we look for lesser meanings. Surely Jesus did not mean for us to literally "turn the other cheek" or to throw our hands, feet, and eyes into the fire if they defile our bodies. Surely He would never invite His people to take a stand that would result in persecution. Surely He would never ask us to give up our rights to sue for damages. Surely Jesus could never mean that our forgiveness from God was directly linked to our forgiveness of others. Surely Jesus did not mean that a glance at a naked woman in an "R" rated movie was the equivalent of violating the marriage covenant. But you see, that is exactly what Jesus meant. Either Jesus said things He did not believe – in which case, He was only the equivalent of many modern preachers – or He spoke the truth and took the message of truth very seriously. If the former is the case, then how can we believe anything He taught, including messages of heaven and salvation? If the latter is true, how can we not obey?

From the very beginning God has called a people to be set apart from the world. Abraham was called out of the caldron of humanity; the Jews were called out of Egypt; and the Christians were called out of the world. We are to be set apart, different from the world around us. We are to care deeper, love more profoundly, obey more perfectly, and serve more diligently than any other people who have lived on the face of the earth. The key phrase of the Sermon on the Kingdom Road may be "do not be like them."[1] To the crowds Jesus preached repentance and healing, but to His disciples, to each of us who call ourselves Christian, He preached that we are to be different from the world around us. He called us out of the world so that we could stop the decay in the world. He called us to be light to shine in the darkness that surrounds us.

Thus, the Sermon on the Kingdom Road becomes the charter of the Christian faith, the divine link between truth and life. It instructs that we are to be different from the world, different from the nominal church, different from the religious and the irreligious alike. We are the sojourners on the Kingdom Road. The Sermon on the Kingdom Road is the divine link between our creation by God and how we are to live our created purpose. Here is to be our value system, our ethical standards, and our attitude toward money, self-esteem, and relationships. And as strangely and harshly at odds with the world as these teachings may be, as disciples, learners, apprentices of Christ soon learn, the journey on that road is the most fulfilling journey of eternity.

So Jesus withdrew his disciples to continually teach them, beginning with the Sermon on the Kingdom Road. And many disciples followed him for a while. They even did missionary work and performed miracles (see Luke 10). But in the end, the teachings of Jesus were too hard, too restrictive, too demanding, and too offensive. At Capernaum, after an impressive miracle and a particularly difficult teaching, some disciples told Jesus, "This teaching is too hard, who can accept it?" and many of them left Jesus (see John 6). Jesus then asked the Twelve, "Do you want to leave me too?"

His message has not changed. He still yearns that those who are "called" be holy, set apart, and different from the world. His question remains, two millennia later, "Do you want to leave too?" Peter's reply is the only reply a Christian can have. "But Lord, where would we go? Only You have the key to eternal life." (John 6:68). And we must know that eternal life begins in Christ, and it can begin today.

The dots are readily connectible. The beginning dot is where we are. (Remember the signs in the shopping malls – "You are here!") The final picture is the Kingdom of God. To make our lives Kingdom lives, we must walk on the Kingdom Road. And as we connect dot after dot in our lives, the transformed image of the King will begin to appear in us.

Part I

Planning the Trip
The Beatitudes

Chapter 2

The Only Way to Happiness

Blessed are the poor in spirit, for theirs is the kingdom of heaven. Blessed are those who mourn, for they will be comforted. Blessed are the meek, for they will inherit the earth. Blessed are those who hunger and thirst for righteousness, for they will be filled. (Matt. 5:3-6)

Where are you now? What is your beginning point? What are you looking for in life? For most people, even most Christians, we are simply trying to get through this life, loving our families and friends with some degree of material success and the least amount of heartache. In short, we are just trying to be happy.

We humans seek happiness above all else. We seek it in relationships, in possessions, and in experiences. These desires are not evil or degrading. Indeed, our deep desires for joy and happiness are actually gifts from God to cause us to turn our faces toward Him. David wrote, "Delight yourself in the Lord, and He will give you the desires of your heart" (Ps. 37:4). Maybe this passage more than any other drove Jesus to open His Sermon on the Kingdom Road with a discussion on happiness. God wants us to be happy. He goes to extraordinary lengths to show us how. But be prepared, this happiness will turn your world upside down. It is not a broad, inviting, and easy road that Jesus invites us on. It is a road filled with steep grades and narrow passageways. It is guarded by a gate that you must walk through alone. It is a road that will often make no sense, will seem out of touch, and will require too much. But given a chance, the journey on this road will cause us to find that which we seek. Consider the things that Jesus called "happy."

Poverty of Spirit
"Blessed are the poor in spirit, for theirs is the kingdom of heaven." (Matt. 5:3)

Let me tell you where I was when I embarked on the *journey*. I will never forget that morning. It was a particularly beautiful spring morning in one of the most beautiful spots on earth. Behind me were the foothills of the Teton Range. The sun was just beginning to glance off the peaks. Snow was still abundant in the high country, but down below the green grass had begun to peek through the patches of white. Heavy dew coated the meadows that gathered the light in a splendid array of color. Patches of fog ruled the valley as it quietly serpentined down the Snake River.

As I got into my Bronco that morning, life was good. Margaret and I had just recently celebrated the marriage of our oldest daughter. Our middle daughter seemed to be making her dent in the world, and our youngest was a junior in high school. This meant that my wife and I could now experience time together unlike any other time in our 23 years of marriage. Business trips, which had to be made alone for so many years, could now be shared. We were planning a romantic vacation, and my consulting business was doing well. Life just seemed to be balanced for the first time. Maybe after so many years of wandering restlessness, we had found a home.

Traveling out of the housing development known as Rafter J, I drove past the small development office, which also served as the post office for residents. Just as I drew parallel to that building, for reasons I will never fully know, from down deep inside my soul came a primordial scream, "God help me." I pulled over and wept as I have seldom wept in my life. It was a deeper cry than when my father or mother had died. It was a deeper cry than when I had to leave a business I had once cherished. It was deeper than anything I had ever experienced.

I had always considered myself to be a Christian. Certainly I was not walking on the Kingdom Road (I did not even know about it), but I knew few who really were. No, I was just another person who called himself a Christian. I even went to church on special occasions. I was baptized and had my children baptized. I despised "going to church" because "I could get closer to God with a fly rod in my hand than by being among the hypocrites." I had been taught since a small child that Jesus died for my sins, but I had no idea what that meant. The stories of the Bible were familiar to me, but the context and the meaning of those stories did not seem relevant to my life. I knew God performed miracles in the past, and through my beautiful daughters, I had even seen a few miracles myself. But God was not relative to my world-view. He did not enter my decisions, nor did He influence my behavior. He placed no particular demands upon me except to live in such a way that the world was not harmed by my life — that meant integrity in business, semi-purity in speech, and doing nothing to harm my family. But, if those things were violated, God did not really care. My priority setting never included Jesus Christ. Devotional time meant listening to motivational tapes by noted business leaders and pop philosophy "gurus." In short, I professed Christianity with my mouth, but I was far from the Kingdom Road.

My faith was syncretism in the highest order – a little of this religion, a little of that philosophy, and a whole lot of my own opinion. One particular symbol of my synchronized faith was a quote from the book, *Jonathan Livingston Seagull*. The occasion was when Jonathan, having just achieved a higher level of flight than other gulls, flew next to a grand superior gull and asked if he were in heaven. The response was, "Heaven is not a place, and it is not a time. Heaven is being perfect."[1] This quote had become my mantra for life. I had it put in a frame to hang proudly behind my desk for everyone to see. Being perfect to me had no moralistic over-tones, nor did I see in this message any need to find God. It simply meant perfecting my skills and knowledge relative to my career.

Like most families in America, the Bible was part of my library. It even held a distinctive place on my coffee table (I was to learn later that it was intentionally put there by my wife in hopes that someday I might pick it up and begin to read it.). But I was motivated far more by the teachings of the world than by the tenets of God. All that changed that day in Rafter J, when from my inner most being came the scream: "God help me."

I wish I could report that on that very afternoon, I came home picked up the Bible and opened it to the Sermon on the Kingdom Road and my life was supernaturally transformed. But that did not happen. It was several years later before the Sermon became my fuel for life. However, on that day in the Teton Valley, God opened the door for me to find the happiness I had been searching for all my life. You see, on that day I became poor in spirit.

The world, particularly America, is searching for happiness today. Never before in history has any culture been so intent on finding the key to happiness. We are looking for it in possessions, popularity, or in power. We look for it in the things we buy, the places we go, the people we meet, and even in the churches we attend. We look for it in sex, in bars, and in parties. We try to buy that which is not for sale. We try to feel that which cannot be felt. We try to earn that which cannot be earned. The truth is, happiness cannot be bought, felt, or earned, because happiness comes from God and God alone. Any feeling or emotion resembling happiness that does not come from God is a mere counterfeit.

But the real irony of true happiness is that it begins in poverty of spirit. One day Jesus was invited to dinner at a Pharisee's house. As He came in and reclined at the table, there was a loud commotion in the back room. Servants were yelling, accompanied by a loud screech of a very haggard woman of the night. Finally the commotion erupted into the room where Jesus and the Pharisee were at the table. The woman broke free and stood behind Jesus as if for protection. Then to the shock and horror of the Pharisee and the servants alike, she knelt down at His feet, weeping so hard that His feet became washed in her tears. At that moment, the burdens of her life were lifted and joy filled her heart for the first time. Blessed was she because her spirit was made bankrupt by the lies and the circumstances of the world (Luke 7:36-50).

There was once a young man who did it his way. He spent his inheritance on the pleasures of the world. And for a while, he enjoyed popularity and even a counterfeit happiness. But when the money ran out, so too did his friends. His ability to attract women faded as he learned that his popularity was in his pocketbook, not in his charm. With the money gone, jobs being scarce, and hunger setting in, he found a job slopping hogs. It was while he lay in the hog trough, waiting for life to end, that he realized his only hope rested with his father's mercy. On that day, with the smell of hogs freshly on him, he became blessed by the destitution of his spirit (Luke 15:11-20).

Zach was a very small man. He made up for his size with his innate ability to extract taxes from the people, and as a result he was a very wealthy man. For all the world to see, he had it made. But inwardly, he despised his size, and no amount of money could cover that insecurity. So he cheated, he extorted, and he became a dread to those who would otherwise scoff at his size. One day in his sordid life, he learned that Jesus was coming to his town. Maybe it was morbid curiosity or maybe even a glimmer of hope for his black soul that caused him to want a glimpse of Jesus that day. But whatever it was, he became blessed – blessed because the very blackness of his soul, which was there the day before, became cleansed by the power of the One he sought (Luke 19:1-10).

Blessed are those who are bankrupt in their spirits – those who realize that the world with all its lies cannot give us true happiness in life. The world offers a counterfeit because it knows how badly we want happiness. So we strike out after these lies and fill our hands with emptiness. We achieve one level of success only to find that there is only more loneliness at that level. We buy the things we want to buy, only to find we are emptier than when we only dreamed of those things. We fill our free moments with persons, but find that they cannot deliver us from the despair. And after we have used up our power, our prestige, our personality, relationships, and our money, there is no hope left. Blessed are we when we reach that point, because it is at that moment we reach out to God in order to find the only source of meaning and joy in the world.

Happiness from God is so rich and beautiful that we need go nowhere else to find it. Christian happiness is being is such a deep relationship with Jesus Christ that our pilgrimage to find satisfaction comes to an end. We look no farther than the One who took our punishment upon His body so that we might enter into life. And when we find happiness at this level, ours is the kingdom of heaven.

Cursed are the rich, the powerful, and the popular for they seem to be in control of this world, with no thought of the next. But blessed are the bankrupt, the destitute, the undernourished in spirit, because only they realize that in God alone can we achieve the Kingdom of God on this earth and forever. Blessed was I on that day outside Jackson, Wyoming, when God placed upon my heart my total depravity of spirit. Blessed was I when my spirit realized that only in God can I find peace for my soul. Blessed was I that day, when God answered my prayer and sent me on a journey that would cure my restlessness; that would take me away from the philosophers and gurus of this world; that would demonstrate that my joy did not come from living in the most beautiful places of this earth; and that would cause me to give up all I had to serve Him. Blessed was I, because at that moment when I cried out for God's help, He saved my soul and gave me the keys to the kingdom of heaven. I took my first step on the Kingdom Road.

Mourning
"Blessed are those who mourn, for they will be comforted..." (.Matt. 5:4)

A funny thing happens to us when our spirits become bankrupt. We look at the world in a very different way. Things that once we thought were perfectly acceptable become as darkness is to the light. Sin is no longer a word that fundamentalists and preachers use — it defines our lives. Poverty of spirit forces us to see the world around us from God's perspective instead of our own. It demands a recounting of the things we hold dear. It pushes us away from the dinner table of pleasure, self-seeking, and pride. All that is left is the emptiness that sees the lives we have lived as repugnant to the God who wants the very best for us. And when we see our lives and the world from this perspective – we mourn. We mourn for our sins that brought us to this bankruptcy before God. We mourn for the sins of the world, which were once our own. We mourn because we have been a part of the very movement that takes the world in a direction away from God.

Margaret and I drove home from a movie. It makes no real difference which movie. Mostly, they are all the same. Somewhere, even in the best of movies, something is designed to shock the senses of the Christian. This particular movie was clean in language and free of gratuitous violence. But in one scene, two young lovers freely and without constraint of conscience, began to engage in sexual intercourse. There were no scenes of nudity, but the message was clear – when you are in love, sex is the natural expression of that love.

Margaret made the point, "Today, if a family does not go to church there is really no place where a young person hears the message that sex is a gift from God to be accepted as part of the marriage covenant." The real message of media, education, and entertainment is that sex is the expression of fondness. No longer is marriage and commitment held as the ultimate expression. It was on that journey home that Margaret and I realized that the world view we once had no objection to was now breaking our hearts. The "poverty of spirit" which Christ blessed us with now caused us to mourn.

The woman who came to Jesus with anointing oil and a broken heart had a poverty of spirit. A lifestyle of illegitimacy had led her to a poverty of spirit, and now she mourned. The prodigal son, whose spirit was bankrupt in the hog trough, mourned because now, even the servants of his father were more worthy than he. And Zacchaeus, once in the presence of Jesus, mourned the unethical practices of tax collecting that had been so much a part of his life. And they were all blessed, because this kind of mourning was comforted by God. Jesus exalted the prostitute. The father ran to meet his returning son. And the Christ sat at the table with Zacchaeus. Blessed are those who mourn for they will find comfort in the presence of God.

As I look at the grand idea of America and see how we have used the very things that have made us great as tools for destroying our culture, I mourn. I mourn that our rights to practice our religion free of state interference has been perverted to mean practice of state without interference of faith. I mourn that free press, born of the necessity to give us freedom to express healthy views, has been perverted to mean that smut must be allowed to be sold freely on the street corner. I mourn that freedom of assembly has been perverted to mean the right to destroy our symbols of freedom. I mourn that individual freedom has been interpreted to mean a woman's right to choose is more sacred than life created by God in His own image. I mourn that tolerance of others means the institutionalization of lifestyles that are repugnant to God. I mourn all these things and am thus driven to God. And it is only there in His presence can I find comfort, so I become blessed. It is there I realize that God intended government as an instrument for order, not a substitution for Him. So I release my dependency upon government and put my reliance upon God, and there in the ancient path, I find comfort for my soul.

Meekness
"Blessed are the meek, for they will inherit the earth."
(Matt. 5:5)

I will call him William, although I really do not know his name. William was shocked to learn that the good times were over. As the country's leading retailer, he had led a very good life. His company was the icon of success. His stocks were the "blue chips" of his day. For standards of fine linen, there was no place else to go but to William. He had been exalted above all the merchants, but now, Abe told him all that was in the past. Now, at the end of his earthly life, there was a price to pay.

William's problem was not that he was rich. His problem was he was proud. God had given him ample opportunity to use his wealth for righteous purposes. One such opportunity was Russ. Russ had not amounted to much by earthly standards. He had been a janitor in William's factory until he got sick. Then it was welfare for a while, and ultimately he had to resort to begging. Knowing William to be a decent sort, Russ began to station himself outside of his office complex. Each day, as William would walk by, Russ would cry out for help. Each day, as Russ's illness grew worse, he became less recognizable to William and thus easier to dismiss.

Now it was Russ's turn. He was dining with Abe and the others. Russ was now the one dressed in the finest clothes and eating the best of meals. He was the one being toasted, while William was begging from thirst. Why the difference? Why the change?

Jesus told this story of Lazarus and the rich man as a demonstration to the Pharisees who loved money, that kingdom rules were different from earthly rules. In the kingdom, it is the meek and the dependent who are exalted. Those who rely on their wealth, wisdom, and skill on earth, become second-class citizens in heaven. Some even find themselves thirsting in the heat of hell. Somewhere in Russ's life, he must have realized that life was hopeless without God. This created a deep mourning for the sins that consumed the world in which he lived. He mourned that which caused him to beg. He mourned the conditions of poverty, illness, and joblessness. He even mourned his own sins that had separated him from God. And this mourning created in him meekness.

Meekness is that condition a person reaches when he or she realizes that they cannot rely on themselves or on the institutions created by humanity for help. The only One on which anyone can rely is upon God. Jesus understood meekness. It was not a weakness as some thought. It was walking daily, relying upon God for His every action, His every duty, His every thought. As Jesus stood before Pilate, He was meek, not weak. He could have established His throne then and there, but He did not. He let the paltry human institutions condemn Him to death, because He knew that His dependency relied not on the decisions of Pilate or the religious leaders, but upon His Father whose plan was always perfect.

The cross is the ultimate symbol of meekness. The King, who could have stepped down in exaltation, chose to remain there in humiliation until death to serve an eternal purpose. It is in the cross that we understand the blessing of meekness. Because Jesus served meekly on the cross, He inherited the most exalted position in the universe and was given the Name that someday every living creature will bow before (Phil. 2:5-11).

Think about it. In a kingdom where love reigns; where there are no tears, no heartaches, no shattered dreams, who will be the logical rulers? Will it be the ones on earth who made their existence livable upon the trials and tragedies of others? Or will it be those whose lives were lived in service of others – loving them; drying tears, mending heartaches, and building dreams? You see, William could have no part of the kingdom, because he took no part in kingdom principles on earth. He probably would not have even been comfortable living with Abraham and the others. Even in his torture, he continued to exhibit pride.

The new earth will be ruled by the ones, like Russ, who demonstrate the characteristics of Christ. And among those characteristics we cannot escape the reality of His meekness. It is a character formed out of a heart dedicated to God. It is a character that yearns for the things that God wants and cries over the things that God cries over. It is seeing Russ and caring. It is seeing William and witnessing. Meekness is Mother Teresa serving the broken and starving in Calcutta, and meekness is the pastor in the small church in Concrete, Washington, trying to introduce every household to Christ. Meekness is Jim Elliott who understood that "it is no fool who gives up what he cannot keep to gain what he cannot lose." Meekness is Jim Elliott's wife, Elizabeth, who introduced the savage who took her own husband's life to Christ I, for one, am blessed to know that the new earth will be ruled by such as those.

Hungering and Thirsting for Righteousness
"Blessed are those who hunger and thirst for righteousness, for they will be filled." (Matt. 5:6)

One of the most repugnant sights I have seen in a long time was the picture of a "pastor" in Kansas displaying a banner that read, "God hates fags." Let me tell you something that we all need to know. God does not hate anybody. God loves fags. He loves pimps and prostitutes. He loves adulterers. He loves divorcees. He loves gossips. He even loves bigots like the pastor in Kansas. God loves each and every one of them enough to send His Only Begotten Son to die for them. To preach and demonstrate any other message goes against the grain of everything that Jesus lived for, taught, and even died for. A God who hates people cannot be found in the gospel. However, a God who hates evil is found on every page of Scripture.

Evil has many faces. It has the face of bigotry, of hatred, of abortion, of human indifference, and it even has the face of sexual immorality. When we stop and look at the damage those things do to the human spirit and to the kingdom of God, the meek begin to hunger and thirst for the face of evil to disappear. We yearn for a world that is free of violence born of sin. Our hearts pine to see the poster children of starvation with joy in their hearts and food in their little distorted bellies. We crave a world that loves the unborn, who are unseen, as much as the newborn, whom we can see. We even long for a movie where our spirits are uplifted; where God is exalted; and righteousness is considered good.

Jesus tells the meek, happy are you when you become hungry for those things. Lucifer hungered to be God; Solomon hungered for more land, more money, more wives, and more power; Nebuchadnezzar hungered to rule the world; and the rich young ruler hungered to keep his money. But not one of these appetites brought happiness. The devil was cast into darkness; Solomon said it was all meaningless; Nebuchadnezzar grazed with the cattle; and the rich young ruler lost the only One who would have made him truly rich.

I heard an illustration once that was so vivid I will not forget it. (Its source, however, was very forgettable, so I cannot accredit it.) A young man goes to his pastor and confesses that he has been unable to find God. He said he had spent time in prayer and study, but God did not reveal Himself. How could he be sure there was a God when He could not be found? As the story goes, the wise old pastor took the young man into water about waist deep. Then he took the young man's head and placed it under the water. At first the young man waited patiently. But then as his natural urge to breathe became stifled, he began to thrash. Ultimately, the lack of air caused him to flail his arms violently. At that point, the old pastor lifted him out of the water. He asked the young man, "Now do you see how to find God?" The young man, angrily replied, "You almost drowned me. What in the world does that have to do with finding God?" To which the kindly old pastor replied, "What was it that you wanted most when you were under water?" "Air," was the response. "Air was what I wanted most in the world." And then the pastor told him, "When you desire God as much as you desired that air, then you will find Him."

Hungering and thirsting for righteousness is the deep desire for a world filled with the things of God. Righteousness is right loving, right living, and right thinking. So, to hunger and thirst for righteousness is to hunger for the love of God in Christ Jesus to permeate the world for right thinking and to seek to know what that is. It is to thirst for right living and to search God's word to find out what that is. When we hunger for those things we will be filled because those things God so freely gives.

Let's pause for a moment at the end of the first four beatitudes and look at what they are saying. In a nutshell, they are all about God becoming the center of a person's life. Before human relationships can work, before a better culture can be formed, before better governments can rule righteously, God must be the center of the human experience. That is the message of all of Scripture. The first four commandments are all about God – seeking Him, worshiping Him, hallowing Him, and exalting Him. That is what the first three of the six petitions of the Lord's Prayer are all about – God's name, God's kingdom, and God's will. And that is the greatest of all the commandments according to Jesus, "To love your God will all your heart, all your soul, all your mind, and all your strength." So it is no surprise that the keys to happiness in this world must begin with God. The road to happiness is paved with a bankruptcy of our prideful spirits to a point that we know that our only hope rests in God. This moves us to a deep mourning over the sin in our lives and the sins of the world. Thus we become dependant upon God instead of ourselves – even hungering and thirsting for those things that matter most to Him.

Chapter 3

The Only Way to Happiness – Part 2

⋄

If you have been paying attention up to this point, you understand that happiness begins, not with ourselves but with God. Poverty of spirit is an understanding that we will not make the Kingdom of God without Him; we will mourn from poverty of spirit without Him in our lives and in our world; in meekness we allow Him to begin to mold and shape us into a Christ likeness; and we rejoice when we begin to have an appetite for right loving, right living, and right thinking. The first four beatitudes are all about Him. But now our Christ begins to demonstrate how we are to begin our walk into relationships with others. Remember, the Kingdom is about loving God with heart, soul, mind, and strength, and loving others as Christ loved us. That is the map of the Kingdom Road, and the next four beatitudes tell us how to walk on that road. It begins with mercy.

Mercy

"Blessed are the merciful, for they will be shown mercy."
(Matt. 5:7)

Happy are the care givers. Mercy is the natural aversion to everything that is harsh, cruel and oppressive.[1] Mercy is the story of the Good Samaritan (Mk. 10:25-37). You know the story well. This Samaritan, an outcast of Judaism, saw a man who had been beaten, robbed, and left for dead along the Jericho Road. After the Levite and the priest had ignored him, the Samaritan stopped, bound the victim's wounds, carried him to safety, and made sure his needs were met. He was a good neighbor, because he demonstrated mercy.

Throughout the Sermon on the Kingdom Road, we see one recurring idea. Jesus is concerned more about our hearts that motivate our actions than by the actions themselves. What erupts from a character that is right with God, are the characteristics of God. Chief among those is mercy. God is a merciful God. As such He is our model of behavior. As He shows mercy, so too are we to show mercy. In a world that likes vengeance, retaliation, "an eye for an eye," Jesus tells us that God demands mercy.

You want to know what mercy is. Let me tell you about mercy. The psalmist cried out, "Out of the depths I cry to You, O Lord; O Lord, hear my voice. Let Your ears be attentive to my cry for mercy. If You, O Lord, kept a record of sins, O Lord, who could stand?" (Ps. 130:1-3). When we achieve poverty of spirit, we instinctively know that our only hope lies in the mercy of God. Four times in three short verses, the writer calls out, "O Lord." This is a man who understands the need for mercy. I am a man who understands the need for mercy.

If God kept a record of my sins, the fires of hell would be lapping at my feet. If God kept a record of my sins, the burden and the weight of those would crush my bones into a fine powder. If God kept a record of my sins, the list alone would challenge the most sophisticated computer. I understand mercy, because I have received mercy. I can walk down the road, not because I am oblivious to sin, but because God in His mercy has forgiven my sins. I can look my wife and children in the eye, not because I deserve them, but because God, in His mercy has, lifted me out of the miry pit. I can stand in the pulpit on a Sunday morning, not because I am a saint, but because God is merciful.

And Jesus says, "Blessed are the merciful, for they will be shown mercy." That means that to find the mercy of God, I, too, must be merciful. I must reach beyond myself and demonstrate the compassion of God – not to those with unblemished records, but to those who could not stand if their records were weighed against them. Mercy means that I do not condemn the AIDS victims, I serve them. Mercy means that I do not condemn the woman who has had an abortion, but I yearn to help her find peace with God. Mercy means that I don't expel the divorced, but I work with them to be reconciled with God and life. Mercy means that I don't leave fellowship with the adulterers, but witness Christ to them. Mercy simply means that I have compassion as Christ had for the hungry crowds; forgiveness as God had over the psalmist's catalog of sins; empathy as Jesus had for the tax collector; and prayer as Paul had for the churches that rebelled. And I can be happy in that kind of mercy, because then will I receive the blessing of God's mercy to me.

Purity
"Blessed are the pure in heart, for they will see God.."
(Matt. 5:8)

As I sit, hour after hour with grieving families, there is one thing I can be sure of. People want eternity. They may not have given it much thought prior to the death of a loved one, but in the final hours, they want it. They want an assurance that they will see the loved one again. They yearn for hope that will help ease the pain of loss. They even try to convince me that there was something in the character of the departed that will merit them an eternal life. I do not see my job in times like these to cast doubt on the deceased's salvation. I don't tell the loved ones their departed is with Satan now and if they don't clean up their act, they will join them promptly. That may all be true in some circumstances, but I don't believe I can convince them of it during their grief.

But I continue to be troubled. These people are seeking eternity, but not necessarily the Eternal One. They want some kind of assurance that the loved one had fire insurance, but they don't necessarily yearn for the Insurer. All God has ever really wanted from His creation is hearts that seek Him. The reward for that pilgrimage is abundant life on earth and eternal life in His Presence. It seems to me, that the one thing that would give us the most peace in this life would be to see God as He really is. But, you see, that requires something from us – purity of heart.

The word Jesus uses for purity here is *katharos*, the root word of our term "cauterize." Literally, this kind of purity is that which is achieved when something is refined in the fire. Purity is metal without dross; it is water that has reached the boiling point and condensed back to liquid; it is a heart that is transparent before God. I think in the realm of human relationships, purity equates to integrity. Integrity is not a life without sin; — it is a life that yearns to be without sin. Integrity is the same on the outside as it is on the inside. It is a sheet of refined steel, the heart of a hickory tree, the child not yet blemished by sin. Integrity is the church member who weeps before God on Sunday and deals honestly and fairly during the week. It is the pastor who preaches, not as a perfect being, but as a sinner saved by the grace of God. Integrity is the athlete who refuses to take advantage of a blind official and the customer who deals fairly with the merchant. Integrity is the life of Christ lived out in the life of those He has saved.

Dan had this kind of integrity. In his day, he was the essence of the kind of integrity that Jesus called for. This was brightly illustrated in the midst of his personal hardships. Some said Dan had been born with a silver spoon in his mouth. He did, after all, come from the finest of families, was materially well off, and was well educated. But one day, Dan and some of his cohorts became part of a great captivity that interrupted the lives of many their age. They were ushered off to a new nation, not as slaves, but to be part a grand experiment.

Upon arriving in the new kingdom, Dan and others faced many challenges that flew in the face of their heritage and their faith. First their names were to be changed to reflect the new culture in which they found themselves. Then, they were to receive the finest education the dictator could offer. And finally, they were to eat daily at the table of the ruler. But you see, there was a problem with what the world would have called a "great deal." Dan's name was very important to him. Not only was it given as part of his family heritage, it defined his relationship with his God. Dan or Daniel means, "a judge of God." And his eating habits – they were also a definitive part of his relationship with God. To defile himself with unacceptable food would have been unthinkable. So Dan "purposed in his heart not to defile himself" (Dan. 1:8, KJV).

Integrity is purposing in your heart. Christian integrity is believing in what you do and doing what you believe. That is what Daniel did. As a result of that integrity Daniel lived daily in the face of his God. That in reality is what the Greek text tells us. Seeing the face of God in reality means daily seeing how remarkable God is. And the irony of ironies is that it was Daniel and his three cohorts who lived in integrity. It was they, even under the threat of persecution, who ultimately were the only ones who met the king's high standards. Living a life of integrity is not easy. It wasn't for Daniel, and it won't be for us. It is having high standards and living according to those standards. It is a purity that modern generations find repugnant. However, if you want to live daily seeing how remarkable your God is, purpose in your heart not to defile yourself, and you will see Him face to face.

Peacemaking
"Blessed are the peacemakers, for they will be called sons of God." (Matt. 5:9)

I was about to enter third grade. Even vacationing in my favorite spot in the whole world could not remove the thought from my mind. The public school administration was going to begin football in elementary school. My mind raced, thinking I could be like David, Bill, Bob, and Durwood – my older cousins who were already high school football heroes. When I saw myself dressed in uniform, I didn't look like the pudgy freckled faced third grader, with an old leather helmet and cardboard shoulder pads. I looked just like Bob returning the kickoff for a touchdown, David running around the end for a big gain, or Bill bulldozing his way for a first down. Cheerleaders were already draped around my neck, in my little mind.

One of the things I did not envision was that in order to play football, I had to hit somebody. Oh, you don't hit with your fist, but you must fling you body into the opponent's with a ferocity that will cause them to move or fall. That was a lesson I could not quite grasp – a lesson that required me many hours of bench warming to learn. One day it hit me. All of a sudden I had a vision, as vivid as the one in the third grade. I would look beyond a person when I blocked or tackled them. I would drive my body through theirs. And to my coaches' delight, this vision worked. I became a really good football player. I won trophies, received honors, and offered scholarships. I no longer was a pacifist. In fact, some said, I was the meanest man on the team – what an honor.

Football is a great training ground for life. In order to succeed you need to look beyond people. Block them down; tackle them when they try to pass you by. Hit them hard and leave them for dead. Surely I learned my lessons well. By the time I was 25 years old, I was a success. I was the youngest State Parks Director in all the United States. But not only did I achieve that position young – I was good at it. I fired people; cleaned house so to speak, cut careers short, and drove my personnel into the ground. By the time I was 29, I received the highest award my profession handed out. But it did not stop there. A federal agency wanted my talents as a hatchet man. So I kept on driving, hitting, tackling, and leaving my friends and enemies for dead. I achieved high rank in that federal agency, and by the time I was thirty-seven, I had already hit the ceiling in monetary advancement. There was only one thing left – I had to achieve the top spot.

I never got there – God had other plans for my life. But the sad thing is I left many a life in the wake of my ambition. I created work habits in individuals that resembled my own. And when others refused to conform to my style, I cast them aside without thought of their careers, families, or lives. Surely, the person I was would never be called a son of God. You see, I was everything that was opposite of a peacemaker.

In fact, peacemaking is not our nature.

Notice the recreation we indulge in - boxing, wrestling, football, basketball, and even golf. All of these involve conflict. We must defeat the enemy in order to exalt ourselves, and we must exalt ourselves in order to win. Peacemaking "just ain't natural." Yet, the Kingdom Road to happiness requires that we be peacemakers. The Bible is serious about peace. Over 400 times "peace" is referred to in a positive manner. Peace is walking with God, because He is the Prince of Peace, the God of peace.

The world at large has a terrible record of peacemaking. Every war ends in treaties, and almost every treaty has been broken by war. If you have ever been to Washington, D.C., you will find a monument of peace constructed after every war. Someone once said that peace in the world occurs when everyone stops to reload. But regardless of past failures, the Kingdom Road demands that we be the peacemakers of our generation.

Conflict is the opposite of peace, and we must know that all conflict originates from sin. Any attempt at resolving conflict (restoring peace) will always fail if the original cause is not dealt with. Look for example at the riots at Watts during the 1960s. After the riots, our government rushed in to the rescue. They tried to provide jobs, restore dignity, create livable housing, and give money to those in need. Three decades later, after billions of dollars in expenditures and tireless human effort, Watts once again broke out into riots. The reason is simple. The cause of the riots was not need, jobs, or racism – these are only symptoms of the cause. The cause was sin, and sin was the one thing the well-meaning government could not deal with.

Peacemaking must begin with examining the original cause. A husband and wife do not live in peace when sin invades their marriage. We try to restore marriages by changing behavior, but that cannot happen until we change what causes bad behavior. Families live in conflict because sin invades their microscopic culture. Communities live in conflict because of sin. States and nations live in conflict because of sin. Sin invades and distorts reality. To be a peacemaker, sin must be dealt with. And that is not an easy task. It is not easy, because we are all sinners. So to be a peacemaker we must deal first with our own sin, and when we do that, we truly become children of God.

Abraham Lincoln was a peacemaker, and even though it cost him his life, our nation was restored. Jimmy Carter became a peacemaker after he left the most powerful position in the world, and he has achieved more public acclaim than he ever dreamed of as President. Mother Teresa was a peacemaker, and the world saw peace as it was meant to be. I was blessed when I learned that peace with honor is greater than victory in shame. I was blessed when I learned to take the blows that were meant for others. I was blessed when I learned I could win without others losing. And I was blessed when I learned that the good of God is better than any selfish goal achieved. Although I still do not at times look like a son of God, Christ is performing a good work in me as an adopted son of the King and will complete it. When Christ is truly formed in me, then I will be like Him and will reflect His image as the Son of God.

Blessed Are the Persecuted
Blessed are those who are persecuted because of righteousness, for theirs is the kingdom of heaven. Blessed are you when people insult you, persecute you and falsely say all kinds of evil against you because of Me. Rejoice and be glad, because great is your reward in heaven, for in the same way they persecuted the prophets who were before you. (Matt. 5:10)

Let me conclude with a personal story. I wasn't very popular in seminary. It really wasn't my fault, nor was it the seminary's fault, nor was it the fault of the students who ridiculed me. It was really because I was misplaced. I was an evangelical student in a liberal seminary. They could not understand me, and I could not understand them. I didn't seek out a liberal seminary. I just went to the seminary of the denomination of my youth. Little did I know that the denomination of my youth had rejected the Scripture as the authority for life and faith. I still believed the Bible was the word of God, as do most of the people in the pews of this denomination. But the seminary did not – nor did most of its students. Therefore, I was an evangelical fish swimming upstream against the "post-biblical" current.

My ultimate hurt did not come from my seminary experience however. It came from a seminary associate dean a few years after seminary. The church I was serving could no longer tolerate the liberal bent of the denomination. They had invited officials in to talk. They had signed petitions, written letters, held conferences, and withheld money – all to no avail. This movement was well underway when I arrived at the church, but the seminary assumed that I was the instigator. Finally, the church put its affiliation to a vote and the vote was overwhelmingly in favor of withdrawing from the denomination.

Shortly before the vote, I received a scathing letter from this associate dean, a man I had held in high regard. In his letter he accused me of being the cause of the church leaving the denomination and demanded that as a person of integrity I should return the scholarships I had received while attending the seminary. I was shocked to receive such a letter from a man I considered a friend. I wrote him back, asking for an opportunity to talk him through the realities that confronted me. *He never responded.* I was more deeply hurt by this than by any other event in my ministry. But maybe at that moment I became more blessed than any of my fellow students, because Jesus said, "Blessed are you when people insult you, persecute you and falsely say all kinds of evil against you because of Me."

That event captures the essence of the beatitudes. Happiness comes from sources not even contemplated by the world. Happiness comes from God, even in our persecution. We cannot comprehend this until we learn what it means to live a Christian life. The map for the Christian life – life on the Kingdom Road – is most clearly defined in the Beatitudes.

Chapter 4

Salt and Light

꿏

You are the salt of the earth. But if the salt loses its salti-
ness, how can it be made salty again? It is no longer good
for anything, except to be thrown out and trampled by men.
"You are the light of the world. A city on a hill cannot be
hidden. Neither do people light a lamp and put it under a
bowl. Instead they put it on its stand, and it gives light to
everyone in the house. In the same way, let your light shine
before men, that they may see your good deeds and praise
your Father in heaven. (Matt. 5:13-16)

Through the beatitudes, Jesus has shown us the gateway
into the Kingdom Road. It begins with God, and then
moves to others. We are built like that – to love God and
through that love allow Him to build a character of mercy,
purity, peacemaking, and steadfastness for what is right. Only
then can we find real happiness. You see God takes the surrendered life and molds it and shapes it for His divine purposes.
He will not fully use us until our characters are formed.

And do you know what? Character matters. It matters to
you. It matters to your family. It matters to your church and
community, and it matters to your nation. Most importantly,

your character matters to God. Character is a mirror that reflects the life of the individual. And any family, church, community, or nation is a collective reflection of individual character. Sometimes that mirror is a very scary thing into which we look.

Elijah was one of God's great prophets. Elijah, like all of us, had numbered days upon this earth. Even in his great life of service to God, there was a time when he had to go. The story of his passing gives us a real glimpse into the issue of character. When his ministry was over, God simply carried him away. To his intern, Elisha, it must have been a frightening thing to take over such an awesome task as walking in Elijah's sandals. But that is what his job was. So his request of God was that he be given a double portion of God's Spirit, to enable him to meet the challenges of ministry. This was a bold request, but we must keep in mind that this request was not for himself, but so that he might carry on God's work with the integrity and power of his predecessor.

Scripture tells us that one day Elijah and Elisha were walking along when suddenly a chariot of fire with horses of fire came down, separating the two prophets, and Elijah was swept into heaven. Elisha saw this and cried out, "My father! My father! The chariots and horsemen of Israel!"(2 Kings 2:12) Now at this point, you may be wondering what this wonderful story has to do with character. The answer is, "Everything."

Israel, once a great nation under David and Solomon, in Elisha's day was just a shattered remnant of its past glory. No longer did they rely daily on God for their guidance and sustenance. They relied on the strength of their armies, the number of their horses, and the inventory of their chariots. And when a nation begins to rely on something other than God, then a nation's foundations begin to crumble. That is precisely what had happened to Israel. They were only decades from being a sad page in world history. In the final analysis it was not the armies of the north or the barbarians from the east that sealed their doom. The character of the people of Israel was their greatest enemy. The real protection of Israel was its relationship to God. God was the horsemen and chariots who protected this tiny nation, and when their character was far removed from their God, so, too, was their strength.

The beatitudes are in reality a reflection of Christian character. Christian character is a character reflecting a relationship with God, exhibited in our relationship with our fellow humans. (Remember I said, "The Kingdom of God looks like a place where God is loved with all our hearts, minds, and strength; and we love our neighbors as Christ loved us.") It is Christ who tells us we are to have a poverty of spirit, a deep mourning when things don't go God's way, a meekness of countenance, and a hunger for what is right. It is Christ who tells us that out of that deep relationship with God will flow an even deeper relationship with those around us – mercy, integrity, peacemaking, and being willing to stand up for what is right.

But I have a question for you. How can a bunch of people living by such feeble standards as these have any influence on the world? It seems obvious that the "goody two-shoes" will be pushed around, kicked in the ribs, and spat upon in a "dog-eat-dog" world. Be assured, however, that Jesus did not share this kind of skepticism. It was to a handful of Jewish peasants, somewhere in the Jordan region, exhibiting beatitude character, that Jesus entrusted a gospel that was to change the entire course of human history. They were the ones He called salt and light.

That's the way it is in our modern world. We say: "The beatitudes look too wimpy for us. These characteristics carry no strength against the weapons of discrimination, bigotry, immorality, hatred, and the like. We need the government's force behind us. We need to change laws to fit Christian morality. We need the court systems to read the Constitution from a biblical perspective. Those are the only weapons we can use in this great fight for righteousness. Such things as meekness, peacemaking, and mercy are as archaic as the Old Testament."

We only say those things because we lack an understanding of the context in which Jesus first spoke of Christian character. Those to whom Jesus was speaking were an oppressed minority, living in the midst of political, religious, and economic depravity that we cannot even fathom. Remember, the Romans were the ones who invented crucifixion. Rome was one of the most hedonistic cultures that ever existed. Their rulers ruled with an iron hand and gave no thought to peoples and nations other than Rome.

Human nature has not changed in the last twenty centuries. Technology has changed, but not the unregenerate human nature. Science has advanced, but not the sinful state of humanity without Christ. There have been many external changes, but few internal ones.

When modern liberalism broke upon the scene in the nineteenth century, humanity thought otherwise. They somehow believed that advancement in technology, extended life, and better living conditions somehow equated to advancement of the human nature. Their bubble was burst with two world wars, the holocausts of Stalin, Hitler, Amin, and Hussein. The deep sinful human nature is revealed in the twenty-first century in the holocausts of terrorism fueled by hate, euthanasia fueled by convenience, and abortion fueled by lust. Without the character change that comes from Christ, new evidence will always abound that our human nature is corrupt.

That is why the Kingdom of God is so important. For in the Kingdom, life, nature, and character are changed. Christ's words on the mountaintop, when applied to life, are as necessary today as they were when He first delivered His message. And we who are truly Christian cannot escape the reality – we are the salt of the earth and the light of the world. Disciples (you and I) have been given the great and honorable privilege to preserve goodness, bear witness to the truth, and glorify God, through the same character He expected of His first disciples.

That privilege begins with being the salt of the earth. Today, in our culture, salt is primarily used as a seasoning. But in biblical times its primary function was that of a preservative. It kept food from rotting and spoiling. Without some sort of preservative, food will simply decay into an unbelievable stench. Suppose for a moment, you went on vacation one week last summer. You were going camping and decided that one night you would have a nice roast by the campfire. So you take a roast from the deep freeze and set it on the counter. In your last minute hurry, you forget and leave the roast where you laid it. Because the house was closed up, it got very warm inside. Within a few hours, it had thawed. And by the end of the week, when you returned, it had spoiled and had begun to rot. The horrific odor has impregnated your house, your carpet, your furniture, even the paint on the walls. When you arrived home and stepped inside the house, your failure to store the meat resulted in the very worst of your expectations. A good fire was the only hope.

Now you cannot blame the meat. It is simply doing what unpreserved meat does – it rots. The same is true with the world. When it is left to itself, it will rot and decay. The church, on the other hand (when it is made up of Christians who are the salt) hinders the decay. You see, God intends that the most powerful force of restricting evil is to be the humble, the meek, the merciful, and the peacemakers.

But what happens if we are not salt? Two things, really. First of all, the world keeps on decaying. Since Americans started leaving the church in the 60s the evidence is clear. Crime rates have soared. Sexual immorality is rampant. Violence has become so bad, that the womb and the school house, once the safest places on earth, have become the most violent. Lying and cheating have permeated the highest offices in the land. And we, like Israel, no longer depend upon God for our strength.

However, Jesus says something else happens if we do not carry out the privilege of walking on the Kingdom Road. The decay happens to us. We lose our saltiness. **"If the salt loses its saltiness, how can it be made salty again?"** Now if any of you are chemists, you know that salt will not become less salty. There is only one way for us to lose our saltiness. We must become diluted. When we become contaminated by the impurities of the world, we lose our influence. When Christians become like non-Christians; when we dilute our religion with other religions, with pagan worship, and with false teachings we are so much like the world around us, that we have no ability to impact the world. Then Jesus said, **"[The salt] is no longer good for anything, except to be thrown out and trampled by men."** What a downturn, to change from being saviors of the world, to becoming pavement.

Oh, but the character fueled by the King and His Kingdom is pure and has power. The glory of the Kingdom character is that we become so different from the world that we attract people to ourselves. Deep down inside every human being is the desire to be preserved, and the King demonstrates the only way.

The image of salt is a negative image it stops decay. But it is not enough for God's people to stop evil; Jesus wants us to promote the spread of truth and goodness. He said, **"You are the light of the world."** Light doesn't mean as much to us today as it did in Jesus day. It was a dark world when the sun went down. There were no light switches, no street lights, no neon signs to light the streets. Home lighting was sparse and very costly. So when Jesus discussed light, the people knew exactly what He was referring to. Light enabled them to see where they were going; it was far safer in the light than in the darkness. Light was the power over darkness. Biblically, darkness is used 148 times, and it is always negative. Darkness was the place of evil, deception, the domain of Satan; a place where sin took place. Jesus was betrayed, denied, and arrested in darkness. But light is always positive, and it is always the remedy for darkness. We, then, Jesus is saying, are the remedy for darkness.

To be the light of the world means that we are to shine the light of God's truth on the darkness of the world. Wherever there is false teaching, we are to be there with the truth. Wherever there are lies and deception, we are to shine with the truth. Where evil takes place in our community, we are to stand in that place and shine the light of God. Where hunger, heartache, prejudice, and oppression prevail in our world, the Christian is to be there shining light.

In the seventeenth, eighteenth, and nineteenth centuries, there was a darkness that loomed heavily over the world. It involved the buying, selling, and bondage of human flesh for slavery. Many nations of the world depended upon slavery for their labor force. The slave trade was good for the British economy, and slavery was good for America's economy. It was supported, even by elements in the church. It was not a popular thing to do to speak out against slavery. Yet a lone voice in the British parliament, William Wilberforce, fought valiantly for over twenty years, suffering defeat after defeat, until the slave trade in England was abolished. Shortly thereafter the church was mobilized in America, and Christians began to shine their lights until there came a point where slavery was abolished in America.

The Kingdom of Light is still necessary today. A light that shines mercy, purity, peace, and a willingness to die for truth can penetrate the great darkness that looms over our land. The darkness fueled by inner selfishness needs the light of a relationship with the Holy and Righteous God. The outward manifestation of this darkness can be seen in the closing down of sixty churches in America every month, or the killing of our children in the womb. It can be seen in the flesh peddling, which year after year places millions of our young children in the most hideous kinds of prostitution. Darkness is violence in our schools, violence in our workplaces, and violence in our homes.

Christians, we are to turn the light on. We are the light that stands against the darkness. We are the light that takes God's truth into the darkness of men's souls. We are the light that stands like a beacon on the hill to the Christians of the world who are persecuted. We are to be visible. Where the news media distorts the truth, we are to turn the light on. Where our schools teach science lacking empirical truth, we are to turn the light on. Where the entertainment industry is spewing out the darkness, we are to turn the light on. And when our government practices deceit – when our own government supports the trade of young women, when they support violence in the womb, where they stay silent in the midst of darkness in the Sudan and China – Christians are to turn the light on. When Christians are content to sit in the darkness, it means our light is going out.

Character matters. It matters to Jesus, and it should matter to people who are called by His name. It matters so much that He intends the character of Christians to be the very thing that makes a difference in the world. We are the salt of the earth and the light of the world. When the salt becomes diluted and trampled on, when the light goes out, God is not being glorified. And when God's glory is eclipsed, the only hope for humanity is gone. When we go into the world to stop the evil; when we stand with the light of Jesus Christ illuminating the darkness – it is all to the glory of God the Father. Character matters. Walking the joyous path of the Kingdom Road requires it.

Part II

The Kingdom Road
Matters of the Heart
Life on the Road

༂

Chapter 5

The Kingdom Within

❧

I hope you have begun to see now, that Jesus' intentions are to change us, to take us from where we are to where He wants us to be. He doesn't much care about our outward appearances, our successes, our circumstances. He cares about those things that can fulfill us, who are part of His Kingdom, in order to further that Kingdom. Therefore, after showing us how to get into the Kingdom, and how to live in that Kingdom, Jesus begins to show us how life in the Kingdom works. Again, Jesus challenges conventional wisdom. Life on the Kingdom Road is all about the condition of our hearts.

Religions historically have attempted to change people from the outside in. They make laws, tenets, and dogma, and then lay them on the people. Some say eternal life is vested in these external things. Laws are held over the head as a threat, with damnation being the penalty for disobedience. Thus adherents to the religion can never be quite sure of their eternal lives. Do you have to be as good as Mother Teresa to be saved? Or can you be just a little better than Adolph Hitler and make it? One result of this view is that many individuals go through life giving up on eternity and trying to find joy in this life. And often that quest for satisfaction ends in the abuse of others and disregard for the laws which hold a culture together. The other alternative is that people live in quest of that eternal life and become legalistic, rigid, joyless, and always unsure if they have been good enough.

And for the legalists, Jesus said, "*Do not think that I have come to abolish the Law or the Prophets; I have not come to abolish them but to fulfill them. I tell you the truth, until heaven and earth disappear, not the smallest letter, not the least stroke of a pen, will by any means disappear from the Law until everything is accomplished. Anyone who breaks one of the least of these commandments and teaches others to do the same will be called least in the kingdom of heaven, but whoever practices and teaches these commands will be called great in the kingdom of heaven. For I tell you that unless your righteousness surpasses that of the Pharisees and the teachers of the law, you will certainly not enter the kingdom of heaven*" (Matt. 5:17-19).

So, if you are a legalist, beware of Christ's words, because the Pharisees were very righteous people. They prided themselves in keeping over 600 of the some 633 laws. They were, by all historical accounts, some of the most righteous people to have ever lived. Therefore, if you choose the route of trying to get into the Kingdom from the outside in (transforming your character by obeying the law), you have your work cut out for you. You must be better than the Pharisees.

You see, Jesus knew it was impossible to keep all the law, so He ushered in a new standard. Kingdom living must come from the heart and work its way outward. Our obedience must come from a heart committed to God or Kingdom righteousness will not occur. When the Kingdom within is at work in us, then the law is obeyed, not out of legalism, but out of a much higher love. And that is all because Jesus did not come into the world to offer up another religion. He came to offer us new hearts, a new life, and a relationship with the King.

Matters of a Murderous Heart

"You have heard that it was said to the people long ago, 'Do not murder, and anyone who murders will be subject to judgment.' But I tell you that anyone who is angry with his brother will be subject to judgment. (Matt. 5:21-22a)

The Kingdom is a world upside down. This world in which we live is only a negative image of the real thing. Even the way we look at the law is different. Take the Ten Commandments for example. What I am about to say may shock you, but its true. The Ten Commandments are the rock bottom of morality. They are the edge of the precipice before you fall off. They are God's bottom line. If you don't murder, don't commit adultery, don't steal, etc., you are just going to barely make it into the Kingdom of God. If you don't worship other gods, if you don't make graven images, if you don't use the Lord's name in vain, and if you worship every week – you have missed the point. The Pharisees missed the point. To them, being obedient to the law was more important than a relationship with the God of the law. Let me illustrate.

Have you ever noticed that the opinion of those who write the laws is always subject to the interpretation of those who interpret and enforce the laws? I confess, I was once a Pharisee in the federal government. In 1961, the Congress passed a very far- reaching law dealing with how commercial operations should operate in national parks. In reality, this law merely codified a long- standing and very effective policy of the National Park Service to attract private investments in the parks without cost to the taxpayers. It also contained certain protections for those who invested the money. This entire piece of legislation, which spanned years of successful practice, and months of Congressional debate and wisdom, was contained in its entirety on one page. Then along came Pharisee Surles. My staff and I developed a several hundred- page manual for the implementation of that simple law. We told the people what Congress really meant.

You see, that is precisely what the Pharisees of Jesus' day did. Jesus Himself was the author of the law, yet it was the Pharisees who tried to tell Him what the law really meant. In fact, they had written volumes that expanded on the simple command, "You shall not murder." It was they (in their own opinion) who really knew what God meant when He wrote the law. But Jesus told them, "You have missed the point entirely." Take murder for example. What causes murder? If you stick a thorn in your hand and you do not remove it, chances are your hand will become infected. This infection, if not treated, may cause the loss of the hand or even life. Jesus makes it clear, that is the impact of anger in our lives. If we do not remove anger, then the infection of hatred will set in, and when hatred begins then you can count on lives being lost.

The final death count of 9/11 was over 3,000. There were probably more. Pain, heartache, and agony were the life of the innocent and impacted families. Because of this, pastors were asked many questions. We were just as clueless as the inquirers, but we shook our heads and nodded anyway. There was one question, however, I heard more than most. "Why did God allow this to happen?" They asked that as if I, of all people, had an answer. But actually, I do have an answer (or actually, Jesus has an answer). The answer lies in the heart. In fact, most of the problems that we face in our world begin in the heart. Jesus tells us that murder begins in the heart; adultery begins in the heart; divorce begins in the heart; lawsuits begin in the heart; revenge begins in the heart; and discord between brothers begins in the heart. Sin is a matter of the heart.

Let's focus on murder for a moment. Jesus said, "You have heard it said to people long ago, 'Do not murder, and anyone who murders will be subject to judgment.' But I tell you that anyone who is angry with his brother will be subject to judgment" (Matt. 5:21). In those times, the Pharisees were the keepers of the religious keys. And they constructed God's intentions into a convenient code that conformed to their own lifestyles. This was true of the sixth commandment. They had restricted this commandment to the act of homicide. In their opinion, if they refrained from homicides – the taking of life without cause or process — then they were obedient to that command. So, according to their interpretation, "if I don't murder, I don't sin." See what I mean? The command is rock bottom.

Jesus never was satisfied with rock bottom morality. He wanted a people, a Kingdom, who saw beneath the veil of the law and looked into God's heart. God wants His people to love one another as Christ loved us. That means any act of aggression, either verbal or physical, is a violation of God's plan for us. Jesus knew that if we go around saying bad things about people, bad things will happen. He knew that if we feed a sinful heart with murderous ideas, then murder will happen.

Have you ever seen a razorback hog? This wild pig roams the forests of the Southeastern part of the United States. They are so skinny and malnourished that their spines protrude in a grotesque manner causing them to resemble the teeth of old sheep clippers – thus the name razorback. Who would have ever thought that a dispute over one of these wild pigs could result in bloodshed? But that is exactly what happened.

The Tug Fork River flows through a beautiful valley, barely known by the rest of the United States. On one side of the river is Kentucky and the other side, West Virginia. In 1878, two farmers — William and Randolph – had a dispute over the ownership of two of these razorback hogs. Words of accusation became so harsh, the issue finally went to court. But as in the case of most court decisions, the decision leaves someone angry and bitter. Randolph became livid when the decision went against him. Shortly thereafter he set up an ambush against some of William's kinfolks. Shots were fired, but no one was killed. A few days later, however, William returned the favor, having his clan fire upon Randolph's men who were deer hunting in the nearby woods. This time they were not so fortunate. One was injured and another was killed.

As the next four years passed, anger and violence increased. Then in 1882, after an election where the whiskey was flowing freely, one of William's sons was attacked, stabbed 26 times and then shot in the head. His other sons retaliated. They tied three of Randolph's boys to a pawpaw bush and then filled them with 50 bullet holes. By now most of you recognize the feud between William Anderson Hatfield and Randolph McCoy. By the time this feud was over, — 10 men and two innocent women had lost their lives. On top of that another McCoy was sentenced to death and, in violation of state law, was hanged in a public execution. This was a warning of what happens when a human's anger gets out of control.

Scripture tells another story of a murder that began with anger. In fact, it was the first act of violence of one human being over another. Cain and Abel both gave an offering to God. Because Abel's offering was pleasing to God, Scripture tells us that Cain became angry. And when Cain allowed anger to settle in his heart, murder was just around the corner. You see, that is precisely what Jesus is saying about murder. As long as we harbor anger in our hearts, murder will happen.

If we are going to avoid murder, we must understand the cause of murder. Jesus said, "You have heard it said to the people long ago, 'Do not murder, and anyone who murders will be subject to judgment.' But I tell you that anyone who is angry with his brother will be subject to judgment" (Matt. 5:21).

But to understand fully what Jesus is saying, we must first understand two basic concepts. First of all, we must understand the value that God places on human life. In the Old Testament we read that human life is so precious in God's sight that when a life is murdered – which means literally to take a life unjustly – by man or beast, the killer must be executed (Gen. 9:5-6). And the reason is clear – the life has been created in the image of God. When God creates a life, no person has the right to unjustly take that life. But God's meaning goes far beyond that. You see, the law says we shall not take a life unjustly, but God's meaning is that He has placed the welfare of our brothers in our keeping. We are our brothers' keepers. And their life and well-being has been placed squarely in our hands.

The second concept in understanding Jesus' words deals with the meaning of anger. Obviously Jesus is not saying that all anger is sinful, because on two occasions Scripture records Jesus as being angry (Mk. 3:5; John 2:16). So if all anger was sin, then Jesus sinned – a condition we know is impossible. Anger is really divided into two categories – righteous and unrighteous. Righteous anger is what Jesus expressed in the temple and in the midst of the Pharisees. It had to do with God or His character being desecrated. Always this righteous anger is directed toward sin. When we see a child or spouse being abused, we have a right to be angry. When we see drug pushers freely walking the streets of our community while our children are at risk, we have a right to be angry. When we see the wanton slaughter of the millions in the Sudan only because they are Christian, we have a right to be angry. If Christians were never angry at sin, then sin would always prevail.

On the other side of the divide is unrighteous anger. Unrighteous anger is the anger expressed toward another human being. It is selfish anger. It is the anger that comes from someone abusing us. Never is this kind of anger allowed. When God's temple was abused, Jesus became angry. But when He was beaten, mocked, spat upon, and executed, – never once did He express anger. Only words of love came from His mouth. Unrighteous anger is malicious anger, selfish anger, and anger of pride, vanity, hatred, and revenge. And while none of these may actually bring murder, because they are directed at someone created in God's own image – they are tantamount to murder in God's sight. I think John sums it up well when he told his church, "Anyone who hates his brother is a murderer..." (1 John 3:15).

So then Jesus tells us that we not only must avoid murder, we must avoid the very anger from which much murder springs. There are two ways He tells us to do that. First, we must tame our tongues. He said, "... Anyone who says to his brother, 'Raca' is answerable to the Sanhedrin" (Matt. 5:22). "Raca" is a word that is derisive to a person's intelligence. In our modern terms, it is equivalent to calling someone a nitwit, nerd, or idiot. And then He said, "But anyone who says, 'You fool!' will be in danger of the fires of hell" (Matt. 5:22)." A fool in most cases in the Bible is a person who is not right with God. And since only God knows the condition of the human heart, – only God has the right to pronounce such judgment. But, sometimes we get so hung up on the specifics of what Jesus said, we fail to see His intent. When we examine the biblical admonitions on the use of the tongue – how we speak to one another – we see that speaking harshly of another is always condemned by God. Jesus knew that harsh language towards one another would incite hatred, anger, and violence. And where hatred, anger, and violence exist, murder is not far behind.

In the past few decades, we have seen a great deterioration of respectful language. One person's right to speak has become more important than another's right to not hear.

When peoples' opinions differ, civility has been replaced by hostility. The danger in all of that is the very thing that Jesus referred to. We are calling brother's names, and the name-calling will, if not held in check, result in hostility, and hostility will result in the shedding of innocent blood. Our statesmen once knew the art of civil oratory, but now even the highest ranking of Senators readily engage in trashing those whom they oppose. If we do not return to that civility, the Kingdom Road will not be found.

Jesus also tells us that if we avoid murder, we must act swiftly to mellow our anger. He told two parables to illustrate this. First He said, "Therefore, if you are offering your gift at the altar and there remember that your brother has something against you, leave your gift there in front of the altar. First go and be reconciled to your brother, then come and offer your gift." Then He said, "Settle matters quickly with your adversary who is taking you to court. Do it while you are still with him on the way or he may hand you over to the judge, and the judge may hand you over to the officer, and you may be thrown into prison. I tell you the truth, you will not get out until you have paid the last penny" (Matt. 5:23-24). The first illustration is for all whom already claim to be Kingdom people. The parable deals with our relationship one Christian to another. The second illustration is from the law court concerning how we are to deal with our adversaries. The lessons, however, are the same. When we are in dispute with another human being, we are to take immediate, urgent action. Anything else will result in harsh words being spoken; harsh words can result in hostility; and hostility can cause murder. The Apostle Paul put it another way. He said, "Don't let the sun go down on your anger. And do not give the devil a foothold" (Eph. 4:26-27).

There is a crisis of anger in our world. We see it in global terrorism. Anger, fueled by hatred becomes murder – too often mass murder, the murder of multitudes at one time.

We are experiencing a crisis of anger in politics. Anger has become so severe over loss of elections that it is spilled out in deadlock in our Congress. We are experiencing a crisis of anger in our schools, when people who feel marginalized, take the lives of their fellow students in their own hands. And when we experience a crisis of anger, we simply need to expect that murder will happen.

When matters are not settled quickly, the devil is given the opportunity he has been waiting for. Harsh words may be spoken. When these words are spoken, anger abounds. And inevitably, when anger abounds, human life will be lost. And when that happens, judgment is at hand. God is serious about human life. Murder is a terrible crime. Human courts can only intervene when the act is carried out – but God knows our hearts, and it is there He passes judgment.

Matters of the Faithful Heart

"You have heard that it was said, 'Do not commit adultery.'
But I tell you that anyone who looks at a woman lust-
fully has already committed adultery with her in his heart.
(Matt. 5:27-28)

One thing is clear. Our hearts are very important. The heart is both a delicate and a powerful organ. It is delicate in that it holds the key to life. It is powerful in that it propels life sometimes for a century or more. But when the Bible speaks of our heart, it seldom speaks of the delicate and powerful organ that propels life. It speaks of character and being. It is the innermost quality of a person. The heart dictates the quality of person we are. So, just as the heart organ must be nurtured and cared for, so, too, must the inner heart of Scripture.

The tongue is also a powerful instrument. A righteous tongue is choice silver (Prov. 10:20). The tongue has value. But Jesus says that whatever the tongue speaks is merely an overflow from the depth of our hearts. In other words, we merely speak from the condition of our inner being.

Our feet and our hands, they, too, are essential parts of life. It is by our hands that we pick things up to read; turn on television; or carry things into our home. It could be said that whatever is contained in our houses has been brought there by our hands. (Look around, what have your hands brought into your home?) What goes into our mouths touches our hands first. We clean our bodies, and shave our beards or legs with our hands. Yes, hands are very important. But it is the heart that tells the hands what to do. Whether hands are righteous or sinful is not the fault of the hands. Our hands are a condition of our hearts.

And what about our feet? Diligent feet take us to work; lazy feet do nothing. Healthy feet exercise our bodies; but hurting feet stay home. Our feet respond to our stomachs and take us to fine restaurants or to junk food stores. Worshipful feet take us into churches, but the feet of the indifferent take them into bars. However, wherever our feet take us is really a condition of the heart that guides them.

Let me be very delicate for a moment. Our genitals do not have a mind of their own. They, too, only respond to the information they receive. Hearts that are pure pump life into a pure body. Hearts that are corrupt beat vileness that will cause our genitals to sin. Of course Jesus knew that. That is why He spoke in such frightening terms. "You have heard that it was said, 'Do not commit adultery.' But I tell you that anyone who looks at a woman lustfully, has already committed adultery with her in his heart" (Matt. 5:27-28).

Adultery is a three- step process. First, the eyes linger where they should not linger. Remember David? One day he sent all his troops out to war. But he stayed home. Idle time was on his hands. Then with nothing to do, he walked out on his veranda dreaming of the exploits of his youth. The idle time allowed him to indulge his middle- aged fantasies. He probably was thinking, "Oh, how the young maidens used to love me. They sang the chant, 'Saul has killed his thousands, but David has killed his tens of thousands.'" Then it happened. He glanced down from his high porch and saw the beautiful Bathsheba taking a bath. She was much younger than his wives. They were getting old and tired. But this young woman! Oh how pleasing to the eye. Soon the glance became a stare. His eyes rested on what was not his and step one was complete.

The second step to adultery is to feed the mind. The eye that looks at what it should not, feeds the mind with what it must not. The naked body of Bathsheba was like a branding iron upon David's brain. The image was seared into the crinkles and creases. This invading virus silenced David's internal alarms of consciousness and righteousness. Now, David's mind was free to think beyond the boundaries of the narrow road. What would it be like to be with someone so beautiful? Surely she would not refuse a king. How would it feel to have someone so young again? Wouldn't it be enticing to have someone so beautiful to tell his aging life how wonderful he was? These thoughts blew away reason, ethics, and devotion to God. The eyes lingered, the mind raced, and step two was locked in place.

The third step of adultery begins as the messages of the mind begin to flow into the heart. Morality is erased, God is pushed to the back corners, and the corruption of the sinful nature is given a call – front and center. The glance of the eye has turned to a stare; the stare feeds the mind and cauterizes that which is pure, lovely, and noteworthy; the corrupted mind feeds an unsuspecting heart; and now that which was forbidden has become the lust of the heart. And when the heart lusts, adultery is in place. The body will respond.

The Pharisees of Jesus' day wanted to confine adultery to the physical act of sexual intercourse with someone other than the lawful spouse. But Jesus knew that, as hatred was only an opportunity away from murder, so a lustful heart set on adulterous thoughts was only an opportunity away from adulterous behavior. An innocent dinner with the attractive new secretary; choice seats near the cheerleaders; a casual attendance at a movie where nudity and sexual intimacy is explicit; porn sites on the Internet; magazines, magazine ads, and catalogs; and all of a sudden lust begins to infect the heart. No longer does the faithful spouse have appeal. A heart filled with love for family has been infected with a desire to walk on the wide and easy road.

Jesus knew this would happen, so He said serious precautions must be taken. He said, "If your right eye causes you to sin, gouge it out and throw it away. It is better for you to lose one part of your body than for your whole body to be thrown into hell. And if your right hand causes you to sin, cut it off and throw it away. It is better for you to lose one part of your body than for your whole body to go into hell" (Matt. 5:29-30). Now let me be quick to say here that I do not believe that Jesus was into body mutilation. But He was into letting us know how serious it is to allow our bodies to sin. So just as surely as a bullet well placed will stop a beating heart, so, too, will a glance that lingers where it does not belong, infect a righteous heart. And because of that, we must be ruthless in protecting the purity of our hearts.

Sunday School met in the basement of the old First Baptist Church in Cisco, Texas. Mrs. Harrison was my teacher. I had to be good, because her son and my dad were the best of friends. Any irreverent or disruptive behavior would go immediately to ears that would not take kindly to an errant child. But I really liked Mrs. Harrison. She loved to teach us some really neat songs. "Red and yellow, black and white, they are precious in His sight. Jesus loves the little children of the world;" "I Wish I were a Sunbeam;" and the list goes on. One song, though, stuck in my mind (and in my teenage years, in my craw). "Be careful little eyes what you see, be careful little hands what you do, be careful little feet where you go. For the Lord up above is looking down with love. Be careful little eyes what you see." That is Jesus' point. "Don't look! Behave as if you have no eyes. Don't touch! Behave as if your hands were amputated. Don't walk! Behave as if you were a cripple."[1] Anything that causes us to sin must be ruthlessly rooted out of our lives. If there is a habit that has the potential for harm, cut it out, and throw it into the fire. If there is a friendship or association that could lead us astray, get out – flee! If there is a pleasure that could lead to immorality, stop, cease, halt – throw it into the fire before it throws you into hell. Nothing is worth sacrificing your relationship with God. Eternity is more important than time; purity is more important than pleasure; sacrifice now is well worth the wait.

But all that raises a question to the modern conscience. Isn't adultery really between the offender and God? Aren't there many causes of adultery that invalidate Jesus' assumption that it is sin in any and all circumstances? Why was He so harsh? Let me explain. People often ask me about the old picture that hangs above my study desk. It portrays a weathered old mailbox, roosting on an iron pipe, leaning steadily to the east. On the side, the faded hand painted words "Marston Surles." Mesquite trees surround it, and the gravel lane crowds against its base. Just to the right of the "n" on Marston is a bullet hole.

That old mailbox was as much a part of my youth as most any other memory. It contained the heartbreak of bills and the occasional joy of checks that would come unexpectedly – as my dad maintained to his dying day – as an answer to his prayers. It was about a quarter of a mile from the house. While she was able, my grandmother made the daily trek to gather its contents. After she was gone, my dad took over. The mailbox, for all its common simpleness, was a source of daily hope and expectation.

I see many parallels between the mailbox and adultery. But before those parallels make any sense, let me introduce another term – covenant. We are a covenant people. Some covenants are written, some are spoken, some are unspoken, but we live our lives daily around the fact that we are a covenant people. Covenants are not contracts. Contracts can be legally broken. Covenants cannot be. They are a reflection of the very character of the people who enter into them. Take the old mailbox for example. My father had a covenant with that mailbox and all who were associated with it. His part of the covenant was to empty it of its contents every day; to make sure it met the legal requirements of the government; and to properly place it where it provided some ease for the mailman. The United States Post Office was part of that covenant. They would deliver mail into that box every day except Sunday and federal holidays – even when Mr. Coats was sick. And all the people who drove down that dusty old West Texas road were part of that covenant. They were to leave it alone so that it could serve its function.

When the rust gathered on the old box's hinges, my father faithfully made the walk to gather its contents. When the letters painted on the side began to fade and the bullet hole shattered the covenant the mailbox had with passers by, my dad was unperturbed in his journey. Oh, his heart broke a little when he thought of an act so careless as to put the bullet hole there, but nevertheless, the hole did not cause him to discard the mailbox for a new one. When Mr. Coats (the mailman) put bad news in the old box, Dad still made his journey; and when the good news came, it was as if that was all the mailbox ever brought.

You see, marriage is like that. It is not just a physical union between two people. It is a covenant so sacred that to violate it changes the very fabric of life – not only the lives of the violators, but the entire culture where the violation takes place. Nothing quite violates that covenant like adultery. Adultery would be my father going to a different mailbox or the mailbox containing someone else's mail – multiplied by a million, million times. Adultery takes the most sacred act that any two people ever engage in and uses it in common ways. Just as the blood of Christ is the sign of the covenant between God and humanity, the blood of the wedding night is the covenant between a husband and wife. It cannot be broken without death. So when we take our free will, combine it with a lustful heart, and deliberately commit adultery, we kill a union that is more sacred than any union outside our relationship with God. It shatters the trust; it violates the commitment; and it breaks the heart. Only a heart that has been hardened by lust could ever violate such a trust.

There are many who would be quick to say that adultery is not necessarily an act of sex, that it may be an outward manifestation of a covenant already broken in other ways. Some say it is an escape from an unhappy situation. Some even call it "a moment of unbridled passion." Jesus said it was none of those things. It is an outward manifestation of a hard and cold heart. After years of being a counselor I will side with Jesus. You see, we always act on our passions. And if our passion is Jesus, we cannot be compelled to violate that passion with an act of human lust. However, if our passion is fulfilling the desires of our bodily wants, then our hearts become hard to those who love us and the One who died for us. And when that happens, we can begin to contemplate the unthinkable – divorce and breaking of the sacred covenant.

That is the heart of the matter. Jesus said, "It has been said, 'Anyone who divorces his wife must give her a certificate of divorce.' But I tell you that anyone who divorces his wife, except for marital unfaithfulness, causes her to become an adulteress, and anyone who marries the divorced woman commits adultery" (Matt. 5:31-32). There are some things that I harbor a deep wish that Jesus had not said. They are really hard teachings. I like the easy ones. Ones like living an abundant life. Or maybe that He will give us anything we ask for in prayer. I especially like the ones about salvation and heaven. But some of His teachings are really hard, and this is one of them. It is hard because marriage has become so routine in our world. It is like the purchase of a computer. You only buy it for meeting needs; you upgrade as soon as it becomes obsolete; and you cast the old one aside because it has lost its value. So to examine marriage through the lens of Jesus' teaching is too difficult for us pastors.

Harold came into the pastor's study and said, "Pastor, I just don't love Monica anymore. She has become a nag; she has no discipline in the use of credit cards; the only time she dresses up is to come to church; she doesn't clean the house; she calls me to bring home 'fast food' as often as she cooks; and we hardly ever make love anymore. No, Pastor, I don't love her anymore, and I want a divorce." Normally such a tirade would be met with a very pious return to the Scripture. A discussion would ensue about faithfulness, covenant, and commitment. But with Harold, the pastor was tempted to another tactic, because, Harold was a major contributor to the church; he served on the elder board; and he had a greater following than the pastor. Then he came into the study with his problem. At these times, the hard teachings of Jesus become really hard.

Jesus wanted to make it clear that to divorce a woman (or man) for any reason other than violation of the covenant through adultery was to cast her aside, make her surrender to her husband's devaluation of her. So Jesus would ask Harold the question, "What about Monica?" Has she lost her rights as a child of God just because she is a woman? "No," Jesus said, "Haven't your read that at the beginning the Creator made them male and female and said, 'For this reason a man will leave his father and mother and be united to his wife, and the two will become one flesh'? So they are no longer two, but one. Therefore, what God has joined together, let man not separate" (Matt 19:4-6). Moses said in Genesis that God created marriage. But Jesus turned up the heat. He said, "Harold, God created your marriage to Monica, and you cannot violate your covenant with her without violating your covenant with God." So Harold the Pharisee (major contributor, elder, and leader), must face the reality, that to trash his marriage for the whims of this world is to invalidate Monica's faithfulness, her surrender of her own well being for that of the marriage, and maybe even her relationship with herself. It is like making her an adulteress and forever her life will be scarred. Then Jesus would tell Harold, the only reason that divorce is on the books at all is because, "Moses permitted you to divorce your wives because your hearts were hard" .Matt. Mt 19:8). Isn't it amazing that Jesus always takes us back to the matters of the heart?

Let me tell you something I believe with every fiber of my being. If we seek God with the intensity we seek the pleasures and self-satisfactions of this world, divorce would be wiped off the face of America. You see, there is no such thing as "no-fault" divorce.[1] Divorce is the result of hard hearts by one or the other or both of the parties. One (or both) members of the marriage are so focused on themselves that they willing violate the covenant. And when that happens, Jesus said, "You violate the life of your partner."

There is a solution to divorce and the devastation caused therein. That is to renew the meaning to marriage. It must be entered into with an understanding that it is a covenant so strong that only death has the authority to violate it. It may be hard to tell that to the Pharisees of our modern generation, but Harold and his peers must know, that if they are willing to divorce their spouses for any and every cause, it is tantamount to violating their lives.

Jesus took marriage very seriously, so it was imperative that He expressed the gravity of the violation of the marriage covenant. It is not to be taken lightly – but very, very seriously. It is a bond for the raising of children, providing joy, companionship, spiritual strength, and deep love. If we take it lightly, then we can discard it lightly. But the damage to our soul and to the lives of those left in the wake is devastating.

Let me close this thought with the story of Peter and Elisabeth. They are one of the most delightful couples I have ever known. They love the Lord with all their hearts, and they love each other with an undying kind of commitment. On one occasion, Margaret and I were visiting them as we were about to embark on a new ministry. We asked them for any advice they might give in helping us in our new ministry. To our surprise, they jumped at the opportunity to do so.

For both Peter and Elizabeth this was a second marriage. From Peter's first marriage, he had two children, who were teenagers by the time of his divorce. Peter was a man devoted to his family, to God, and to the study of God's word. Divorce was the last thing on his heart. But one day, his wife announced that she was leaving him for a teenager. Certainly he had biblical grounds for divorce. Elizabeth, on the other hand, had three children from her former marriage. They ranged from small child to fledgling adult at the time of her divorce. Her former husband abused her incessantly and finally she could take it no more. So here were two lives devastated by the harsh reality of divorce, yet God in His magnificent grace joined them together. But for the next five years, their lives were constant warfare. They were at war with their children, at war with their exes, and at war with the courts which had bought into this no- fault divorce syndrome.

Their advice? Peter said, "You know, Bud, how much Elizabeth and I love each other and how blessed we feel that God has given us a second chance. But we both agree that if we had it all to do over again, we would have tried harder in our first marriage, because only there is there the ultimate fulfillment that God has in store for us."

Matters of a Disciple's Heart

"Again, you have heard it said to the people long ago, 'Do not break an oath, but keep the oaths you have made to the Lord.'" (Matt. 5:33)

Jewelry adorns most Americans. Some of it enhances our appearance; some just makes us look cheap and gaudy. Some jewelry draws attention to our age; still other jewelry draws attention to our family. Some is an outward sign of our covenants with our spouses and our schools, some is just for decoration. You can almost tell when a man is going through a mid-life crisis just by looking at the necklaces and pretentious rings he suddenly begins wearing. Jewelry can be comical to look at or it can highlight beauty in such a way that we are drawn to the wearer. But there is one piece of jewelry that I think we adorn too whimsically. That is the cross.

Men wear crosses on their lapels, women on necklaces and bracelets. It is worn by Christians as an outward demonstration of their faith, and it is worn by non-Christians simply because they think it is attractive. But, I don't believe most Christians and non-Christians understand the significance. Jesus did not say, "Put on a lapel pin and wear it every day." Nor did He say, "Put on a ring, bracelet, or necklace every day to be reminded of Me." He did not have jewelry in mind at all when He said, "Pick up your cross, every day, and follow Me."

The cross was an instrument of execution. And it came as no surprise to Jesus that He would wind up on that cross – executed like a common criminal. So why would Jesus want us to carry around each day an instrument of execution? Should we hold up our pants with a hang-man's noose; drag an electric chair behind us wherever we go; or keep a vial of lethal gas or a syringe of deadly injection tucked in our pockets? What ever was Jesus telling us?

For non-Christians this will make no sense. But even for sojourners on the Kingdom Road, for the answer to make any sense at all to us, we must be reminded of why Jesus was executed. The human reason for His execution was that He refused to deny Who He was – God Incarnate. That refusal was blasphemy according to the codes of the day, and blasphemy carried with it a death sentence. But never be lured into the trap of thinking that Jesus died for human reasons. Jesus died because it was the will of God the Father. From the beginning of creation (Rev. 13:8), there was no doubt in Jesus' mind that someday He would have to descend to earth and become a sacrifice for the sins of the world. There was no other way.

As we wade through the sometimes arduous chapters of the Old Testament, we begin learning of the tremendous preparation that God was making for this singular event of Christ on the cross. The sacrifices, the rites, the rituals, all point to what God would someday do in Christ Jesus. The prophecy, the promises, and the commands were all a prelude to the God who would love us to His own death. Scripture is clear that Christ died on the cross for our sins. He became sin for us so that we might adorn His righteousness.

As Christians we intellectually know that. I knew it for 43 years before God branded it in my heart and mind with understanding. That is God's work, not the work of this book. My prayer for my readers is that God would brand that intellectual knowledge on your heart and make it part of your soul. But be prepared, if God answers my prayer for you, your life will never be the same again. You will know what it means to carry the cross of Christ every day. You see, just as the human reason of the crucifixion was Christ's refusal to deny who He was, so, too, must we be willing to die for the truth that Jesus Christ is the Son of the Living God, God

Incarnate, God the Son. And just as Christ died for our sins, we must also die every day to sin. That means we must lay all selfish desires upon the altar of sacrifice and put them to death – every day. We must live in the reality that God is right and the world is wrong. His word is His promise, and it is always true.

Let me take just a brief moment of your time to review what you have read up to now, so that what I need to say will be in its proper context. The Sermon on the Kingdom Road, as wonderful as the teaching is, is not for everyone. Jesus took His disciples to the mountaintop to give them special instructions for kingdom living. So the Sermon was for His disciples. The purpose was to establish a new order of living, which He would ultimately define as part of the cross carrying. It would be the manifesto for Christian living. It would be the journey that disciples are to walk once they have received the saving grace of our Lord. It is all about Christian character and the consequences of that character. It is about our relationship with God and how that relationship plays out in our human relationships. It is about standing for what is right, good, pure, and lovely and shining God's truth in a very dark world. And as disciples, Christians must not deal from a neatly packaged set of outward rules; we must live in the world with a heart that is transformed by the power and grace of the One True God. Christian living is a matter of the heart.

One of my pet peeves, even when I say it, is when someone ascribes an event or characteristic as the purpose of God. God never does anything singularly. With that said, let me just say that one of the purposes of God for wanting His people to have transformed hearts is that we might make a better world – that we might be constantly at work providing a seed bed of fertile soil in which His word might be more abundantly planted. And if this is important to God, it should be equally important to those who are journeying on the Kingdom Road. As any aspect of life, to do something effectively we must practice it continuously. Cross carrying is a daily exercise.

Jesus gave us some effective cross- carrying exercises. One way we can practice cross carrying is to be people of our word. Jesus told us, "Again, you have heard it said to the people long ago, 'Do not break an oath, but keep the oaths you have made to the Lord.'" (Matt. 5:33). Now, if someone perverts just one part of God's intentions on this earth, beware – they feel perfectly free to pervert them all. The religious leaders in Jesus day were busily warping God's intentions on matters of homicide, adultery, and marriage; they had also conveniently perverted His intentions when it came to oath taking. The rabbis of the day said that oaths taken by using God as a witness were the only oaths with validity. So, the reasoning went, unless you invoke the Lord's name, there was really no reason to be particular about keeping your word.

Now let me ask you, does that sound like something that Jesus would endorse? Hardly, unless you have a very limited view of God. The world and everything in it belongs to God. So it is hardly possible to swear by anything without taking God's name in vain. He said if you swear by heaven, that is God's throne; if you swear by earth, that is God's foot-stool; if you swear by Jerusalem, that is His City; and if you swear by your own body, that is His temple. Simply put, God owns it all. You cannot swear by any creation and not invoke God's name.

But you see, just as people in Jesus' day, we have developed a culture in which people must swear by something. And the reason we must swear beyond ourselves is because we have become so untrustworthy. Cross bearing is trustworthiness in our word.

Let me tell you about my Aunt Tad. I am sure she had her day when the strength of her faith did not attain all that I remember, but Aunt Tad was the most faithful woman I have ever known. Her word was her bond. When she told you she would do something, she would move heaven and earth to fulfill that word. She was faithful, true, and she would never let you down.

Aunt Tad had a ministry (she had many, but there is one I want to discuss).[2] She touched the lives of the elderly whenever she could. She brought them joy every day she had the strength. Up until Aunt Tad was 88 years old, she went to the nursing home twice a week to tell the "old people" the Good News about Jesus. But you know what else she did? She walked two miles every day. The reason she did that was because she knew if her legs went out, she could no longer serve. So every day, until she was 88, she walked her two miles, so that she could fulfill her commitment to the elderly of her town.

One evening, shortly after her 88th birthday, Aunt Tad was leaving a Bible study at her church, and she tripped over a parking barrier. She broke her shoulder. The church scurried around trying to protect itself from a lawsuit. (How little the staff and leaders knew this saint in their midst.) But do you want to know what Aunt Tad did? She said, "This is a sign from God that He wants me to serve the elderly every day." So she checked herself into the nursing home, and there she stayed until she was 97. And she did this because she made a commitment and her commitment was her bond.

Every night, after her beloved Harl passed away, Aunt Tad would pray, "Lord, let me wake up in Your arms tonight." And every morning when she would wake up, she would say, "Okay, Lord, I guess You still have a plan for my life on earth." And she would get up, shower, eat breakfast, walk her two miles, and go to work in serving Him. You see, Aunt Tad knew the Kingdom Journey was the right journey. She found joy in the steps and purpose for her long life. But she also demonstrated another point. She fulfilled her oath. Not by swearing on this or that, but by living her life for the glory of God. She made a commitment, and then fulfilled that commitment, even when it meant walking two miles to keep up her strength, or checking into a nursing home to fulfill her promise. Her "yes" was "yes," but seldom did I ever hear Aunt Tad use the word "no." Oh, how I miss her!

Leading with Your Chin

"You have heard that it was said, 'Eye for eye, and tooth for tooth.'
But I tell you, Do not resist an evil person. If someone strikes you on the right cheek, turn to him the other also. And if someone wants to sue you and take your tunic, let him have your cloak as well." (Matt. 5:38-39)

Nothing is quite so disarming as love. I will never forget the first time I saw her. She was freckled faced, just had a new perm for school so her hair was still frizzy, and she was skinny. But I can tell you, I was totally disarmed. I had no words to say. In fact it took me nine months to pick up the courage to say anything at all to her. I just mooned and pined in love during those times. Finally, at the end of our sophomore year, I picked up enough courage to ask her to our class picnic. If she had said "no," I probably wouldn't be here today. I was disarmed by love.

But I just thought I loved her then. It was a few years later when another kind of love disarmed me. She was holding our firstborn daughter. The baby was only 4 pounds, 3 ounces, and today she would have been held for weeks in intensive care. But in those days, we were pretty much on our own. And I will admit our daughter looked more like a skinned squirrel than a baby. But my beautiful wife held that baby, and the love I saw in her face was unlike anything I had ever seen in my life. I was disarmed by love.

I have had a very healthy life. I avoided hospitals totally and doctors mostly until I was 57 years old. I was so healthy, in fact, that I abused my body with poor eating habits (Mexican food and hot sauce on every possible occasion, chocolate and coconut cream pie as healthy habits, and washed it all down with the wonderful potlucks of our church) and poor sleeping habits. Notice I said, until I was 57. Then it happened. I had begun to feel fatigue as I had never experienced it before. I felt like I was walking in molasses. My strength was almost gone. One night I could barely hold my head up, I felt like I needed at Roto-Rooter in my chest, and antacids refused to help. I stayed silent. But by nightfall the next evening, I knew something was badly wrong. I told Margaret, "I think you had better take me to the emergency room." She screamed, "Oh no!" All of a sudden I felt safer than I have ever felt in my life. Let me tell you at that moment, I was totally disarmed by love. I could tell you many more stories about being disarmed by Margaret's love, but you get the point. Love has the power to totally stop a person in their tracks and hold them completely captive.

Isn't it funny (strange), in all human relationships we don't recognize the power of love to disarm, persuade, and even defeat? We seem to think that outside of family love, we need to deal with all other issues forcefully. Remember the book, *Winning by Intimidation*? That is the way of the world. Overpower, force against force, evil against evil, my rights against your rights, and an eye for an eye – these seem to be the tools for getting what we want. Strangely enough we use these things somehow thinking that we can have peace.

But Jesus says it is love that disarms. There is nothing quite so disarming as the power of love. Suppose for a moment that you re-tool. You drop the weapons of the world – revenge, hatred, and demands for personal rights – and decide to do things Jesus' way. For some reason a person hits you in the jaw. Now if they do that, what they are communicating is that "I want to fight." But suppose, you step up to him and offer your other jaw, and then you say, "Please strike the other jaw so that your anger can be fulfilled." What do you think they would do? Most probably they would become confused and walk away. But even if they did not, their anger would have been disarmed by your love.

You see, Jesus tells us Christians that the most compelling characteristic of the Kingdom of God is love. And His plan is to overwhelm the world with love. Nothing is quite so disarming as love and if we would respond to threats, lawsuits, anger, even violence with love, seen in turning the other cheek, walking the extra mile and giving away our coats to thieves, then the world would begin to see its awesome power. Mahatma Gandhi and Martin Luther King, Jr., brought down powerful human institutions with this concept – and we can too. All we have to do is trust Jesus. Lead with your chin, and you will find out that love is disarming.

Using love to disarm anger, hatred, violence, and oppression may be the single most lacking Christian characteristic, but when it is in existence, when it is manifested in a Christian on the Kingdom Road, the power of the Kingdom begins to show forth. And because of our innate defensive mechanisms, this may be the hardest characteristic of the Kingdom to make real. Nowhere in all the teachings of Jesus, must the sojourner call upon His power to make this real.

But it can happen. Jesus proved it. The guards spat on Him, mocked Him, struck Him in the face, and then put a crown of thorns upon His head. His response? "Father, forgive them for they don't know what they are doing." The religious leaders jeered Him, lied about Him, and even denied the Father as their King, and it was they who screamed, "Crucify Him," who was innocent, in trade for one who was a hardened criminal. His response? "Father, forgive them for they don't know what they are doing." Even His disciples ran away. One betrayed Him. One denied Him, and all abandoned Him. They were all cowards in the moment of His greatest need. His response? "Father, forgive them for they don't know what they are doing."

There was a Roman soldier at the foot of that cross. He was disarmed by Jesus' love. He went from being party to driving the nails, casting the lots for Jesus' clothes, for hoisting the massive cross into its socket, to being humbly disarmed by the love of the man on the cross. Whenever love is practiced in the way it was taught, you can be assured it will be disarming.

But there is a problem. We are to share in Christ's way of doing things. Peter said, "To this you were called, because Christ suffered for you, leaving you an example, that you should follow in his steps" (1Pet. 2:21). Participating in Christ means following in His steps, and following in His steps means participating in His suffering. And participating in His suffering means we must be willing to participate in the consequences of love. As sojourners on the Kingdom Road, we are called to be peacemakers, and real peace cannot even begin outside the disarming power of love.

Do I believe that war, terrorism, oppression, and abuse could end if we practice love? No. But I believe the world would be a whole lot better off if we who are Christians would behave in the manner to which Christ called us. Jesus Himself said there would always be war. However, Paul makes it clear, "As far as it depends on you, live at peace with everyone" (Rom. 12:18). You see, we are not responsible for how people react to our obedience, we are only responsible for our obedience.

So, the next time somebody shoves you, let them shove you again. Sometime when labor wants a $1 raise, give them $2. Sometime when management wants you to work an hour extra, work two. The next time somebody cuts you off in traffic, pull over and pray for them. The next time somebody takes away a customer, recommend another customer to them. Sometime when someone takes you to court, ask them into your home and see if there is anything else they would like. Lead with your chin and see what happens.

Maybe nothing. But what if we Christians were known for that lifestyle?

You see, there was a time when we were. It was about 1700 years ago. There was a co-emperor of Rome named Constantine who refused to persecute the Christians, although that was the order of the day. He would not, because he was disarmed by their love. And when Constantine became ruler of the world, and in the process becoming a Christian himself, Christians were set free from persecution and the visible Church grew in status, second only to the Empire itself.

However, Christians made a fatal error. Once they gained power, love became secondary, and we have watched 1700 years of decay and erosion. Only love will disarm, only love will sustain. Only love will endure. Love is the pavement on the Kingdom Road.

Chapter 6

Kingdom Intentionality

❦

"Be careful not to do your acts of righteousness
before men . . ." (Matt. 6:1)

Why do we do the things we do? This is the ageless question. And for those who desire to live on the Kingdom Road, they find this the most perplexing question of all. Take Paul, for example. He wrote, "I do not understand what I do. For what I want to do, I do not do, but what I hate, I do" (Rom. 7:15). These are some of the most comforting and, at the same time, frightening words ever written. They are comforting in that we know that even the Great Apostle struggled with sin, just like you and me. But they are frightening when we learn that even someone as close to Christ as he was, still wrestled with sinful thoughts and desires.

As we walk through this life, stumbling over growing up, marriage, child raising, careers, and retirement, seldom do we really understand why we do the things we do. Young people, why do you participate in athletics, music, or art? Is it to be a star? As you are dribbling the basketball down the court, are you thinking about tomorrow's headlines; are you thinking about the scholarship you might receive; or are you just trying to be the best you can be with the gifts God has given you? Or how about when the baby wakes up at 3:00 a.m.? Young mothers, do you get up and check so that your husband will applaud your dedication to motherhood; are you just reacting to the noise that disturbed your sleep; or are you expressing your love for the precious child God has given you? And what about you farmers? Why do you sit on the tractor all day? Is it so that tourists driving down the road can look at you and applaud your hard work and dedication? Or is it to give glory to God by providing a living for your family, food for your neighbors, and tithe for your church? Whatever it is that we do, we do it for a reason.

The same thing is true for the things we do in our relationship with God. We go to church, worship, study our Bibles, and give our offerings, pray, and fast – all for specific reasons. That is the issue Jesus was addressing when He said, "Be careful not to do your acts of righteousness before men, to be seen by them. If you do, you will have no reward from your Father in Heaven" (Matt. 6:1). Up until this point, Jesus had spent a great deal of time discussing what it meant to be righteous. It is always a matter of the heart.

If that is true, then we can be righteous according to the law and unrighteous in God's sight. Let me give you an example. There is an elementary school behind our church. In the wonderful community in which I live, children still walk and ride their bikes to school. There is at least an air of freedom from the kind of things that happen in the cities. It is fun to watch the precious children making their daily way — walking, riding their bikes or skateboarding to school. On the busy throughway street that runs in front of the school, there is an amber light and a sign that says 20 mph when the light is flashing. Note: The law says 20 mph per hour. Now my question is, are we being righteous when we drive 30 mph through that zone? How about 25? How about 20? How about 15 mph? At what speed do we achieve righteousness?

The answer, according to the law is 20 mph. The answer, according to Jesus however, is that you achieve righteousness, when you love little children enough to drive in the most attentive and careful way as you pass through the zone. Who knows what child may be lurking behind a car to make a run for it? Righteousness is not attained by following the law; it is attained by having a heart for the purpose of the law.

One of the key passages in the Sermon is ". . . Do not be like them." People who walk on the Kingdom Road are to be different from the world. We are to care more, love deeper, and serve more willingly than any other people on earth. And we do this, not so the world will applaud us, but because God is our Father and Christ is our Lord. We are to go through our daily routines of worshiping Him, not so people will find us worth observing, but because our God is worthy of our praise. This is true in giving, prayer, and fasting.

Giving is the first. "So when you give to the needy do not announce it with trumpets, as the hypocrites do in the synagogues and on the streets to be honored by men" (Matt. 6:2). Have you ever noticed how some people make great shows of their giving? Most churches are filled with plaques, in memory and in honor of someone special. Many people take their offerings directly to the pastor so that he or she will know how much they gave. Some hold up the passing of the plate to make a show of writing out their checks.

One day, Jesus and His disciples were in the temple courts. The Pharisees, Sadducees, and the teachers of the law made a great showing about putting their ten percent in the plate. But a poor widow came and gave a pittance. Jesus told His disciples, "I tell you the truth, the poor widow has put more in the treasury than all the others. They gave out of their wealth; but she, out of her poverty, put in everything – all she had to live on" (Mk. 12:43-44).

There is a great debate in the modern church about giving. Some are very legalistic about the concept of tithing. Others say that tithing is the baseline of giving, and is to be only our foundation. Still others, in an effort to be open on the issue, quote Paul: "Give with a cheerful heart, for God loves a cheerful giver." Whatever your opinion, Jesus expects us to give. He did not say, ". . . If you give." He said, ". . . When you give." So giving simply is not a Christian option. However, in this passage, Jesus is not discussing how much to give, He is discussing the way in which we do it. His concern is how Kingdom people do what they do – even giving. For us sojourners, our giving should flow from our understanding of our blessings. Scripture says, "To the Lord your God belong the heavens, even the highest heavens, the earth and everything in it" (Deut. 10:14).

A basic Kingdom understanding lies in that passage. Kingdom people must begin with the foundation that everything we have belongs to the Lord – our families, our homes, our cars, our income, our bank accounts, and our credit cards. Everything belongs to Him. So when we give, we do not reward the church board for a job well done; nor to make a statement on how much we like or dislike the pastor; nor do we give to support the church budget; nor do we give out of obligation to a Hebrew law. We give because what we have belongs to the One to whom we are giving. It is not ours to give, but His from the beginning. And if that is not your motive, then Jesus has some serious words to say. "I tell you the truth, they have received their rewards." If our motive for giving is not to give back what is already His, then when our motive is fulfilled, we already have received our reward. But if we give with a righteous heart our rewards come from God Himself.

After discussing stewardship, Jesus shifts our attention to prayer. "And when you pray, do not be like the hypocrites, for they love to pray standing in the synagogues and on the street corners to be seen by men" (Matt. 6:5). The religious leaders of the day made a big deal out of their prayers. They would literally stand on the street corners and in the temple courts and with their arms stretched to the heavens would cry out their prayers. People would walk by and say, "Wow, what a religious man he is," thus giving the religious man what he was seeking – attention from men.

But to Jesus, prayer was too important to be a ritual or a show. Like giving, our prayer life is a representation of how we view God. Jesus began His day in prayer alone on the mountain tops or along side the river banks; and He would end His day in the same way. His prayer life was a reflection of His attitude toward the Father. He prayed before going into the wilderness. He prayed before selecting the disciples, and He prayed before He went to the cross. Prayer was about His daily relationships, and it was about strength for the journey that lay ahead of Him. That is what prayer is to be for those on the Kingdom Road. Our motive of prayer should be our relationship with our Father in heaven.

We have legalists today who use this passage to try to determine how we are to pray. Some churches refuse to have prayer in church because of this passage; others say prayers should be short; others say the only way we should pray is in the privacy of our personal prayer closets. But that is not the point Jesus was making at all. His point, as in all religious acts, is that of motive. When we pray, we are talking with our God, and it's none of anyone else's business. That doesn't do away with corporate prayer, unless the one praying is praying, not to intercede for the people but to draw attention to oneself. We pray, not to inform God, but to be with God, because He already knows the depth of our hearts.

Then, Jesus addresses the religious act of fasting. "When you fast, do not look somber as the hypocrites do, for they disfigure their faces to show men they are fasting" (Matt. 6:17). Again, He was discussing motive. The Pharisees walked around with long faces, demonstrating how much they were suffering for God. But, as usual, they missed the point. Jesus knew God's purpose for instituting fasting went so much deeper. And what made fasting important in biblical times has not changed. The conditions that existed then that caused people to fast still exist today. Scripture gives us four ways or circumstances to fast. Fasting was used to humble the people before God. When they became distressed over sin in their lives or sin in their nation, they were to weep, pray, and fast. God still intends us to weep, pray, and fast over our own sin and the sin of our land. Secondly, fasting was used as a means for people to express their dependency upon God for future events. When people sought God's direction, they turned away from earthly food and distractions. In our fast- paced world, so filled with distractions from the things of God, we should be more dependent upon God than ever before. Thirdly, fasting was a way to exercise self- control. It demonstrated control over the human nature; and it provided a way to discipline bodies and make them obedient to the soul, not vice-versa. No time in history has humanity been so far removed from self-control. Now more than ever we need to gain control over our bodies and make them subject to God. And finally, fasting was used as a way to do without food, so that what they did not eat could be distributed to those who had none. In our land of luxury, this could be a gentle reminder that we need to share our plenty with those who have none.

In no case, however, is fasting to advertise ourselves. Jesus said, "But when you fast, put oil on your head and wash your face, so that it will not be obvious to men that you are fasting" (Matt. 6:18). Fasting is to discipline ourselves. It is to express our dependence upon God, and when we do that, that is reward enough.

Giving, prayer, and fasting are authentic Christian acts. To give is to serve others with what God has given us; to pray is to seek Him; and to fast is to demonstrate our reliance upon Him. And we are to do these things in secret. Absolute secrecy in these religious acts is not possible, because even if no human is there to watch, God is watching. He is to be the only audience that matters to Kingdom people. So what Jesus was trying to tell His disciples is that we need to become so God-conscious that we cease to be self- conscious. The answer, then, to why we do the religious things we do, be it worship, giving, prayer, Bible study, or fasting, is to intentionally please the spectator who matters most — God is our only audience.

Part III

The Rest Stop
The Lord's Prayer

❧

Chapter 7

Looking Upward

꒜

"This, then, is how you should pray:
Our Father, in heaven, hallowed be Your name;
Your kingdom come; Your will be done; on earth as
it is in heaven. (Matt. 6:9-10)

On the journey down the Kingdom Road, as with any other journey, we get tired and, need a break, refreshment, and renewal before continuing. That is why Jesus suggested the rest stop, which is prayer, and He told us how to use that break most effectively.

Pineapples in the Fire
"This then is how you should pray. . ." (Matt. 6:9)

A new pastor was increasingly concerned about the spiritual health of the congregation. The traditions of the church seemed to be the driving force behind every worship service. His solution was, rather than trying to help the congregation grow in depth and understanding of the faith they professed, he tried to punish them. When he felt the music was stuck in traditionalism, he sold the church organ. When he felt the choir was not performing well, he abolished it. And when he felt the congregation was only giving lip service to the "Lord's Prayer," he removed the liturgy from the service. When questioned about why he was doing that, he answered, "Because they were only throwing pineapples into the fire." His meaning was that the prayer had become a ritual with no more redemptive value than the pagan custom of throwing fruits and vegetables into a fire as ritual sacrifice – an appeasement to the gods. While his analysis may have been correct, his solution missed the mark by a mile. I sincerely believe one of the great gifts a pastor can give to his congregation is a deep and abiding understanding of the Lord's Prayer, for it can never be "throwing pineapples into the fire."

The pastor's statement, in my opinion, was treason against the beautiful and wonderful prayer. For in this prayer lies the key to all relationships with our God and with our brothers and sisters. If we would follow Jesus' teachings here, we would become both personally and as the Body of Christ all He desires that we be, and the mystical transformation of our lives could take place. Please don't believe I have achieved all I am going to write about. Sadly, I have not. But I am at work on it. And I want to share that work with you that we might grow together. I am excited about this journey, and I hope you will prayerfully join me on it. For if we reach together the ends to which Christ called us, we will be a force, wherever we are, in our churches and communities that will transform them for God's great purposes. So buckle up, sit back, and pray.

Our Father

"This then is how you should pray. . . Our Father, which are in heaven . . ." (Matt. 6:9)

The prayer begins in such a way as to shock His listeners. It would have been a shock because the Fatherhood of God was discussed in the Hebrew Scriptures only corporately (e.g., Father of Israel) even then in only a couple of places.

Yet, Jesus was challenging His disciples of the Kingdom Road to personally call God "Father."

At first glance, beginning the prayer in this way, it seems Jesus placed a terrible burden on fathers. When we visit with God, if the image we have in our minds is that of an earthly father, this can be very hard on some people. That was not hard for me. I had the best dad in the world. He was not just a father; he was my best friend all through my high school years. In the summer we went fishing almost every morning (except Sunday of course) and in the winter there was always some critter that needed hunting. He was my greatest fan as I played football. Except for the games that were so far away that he could not make it home by milking time, he was always there. I remember once sacking the quarterback for the second time in a game. Dad was sitting in the press box, and I heard his voice over the loud speaker – "That's my boy." We never talked much about affectionate things, but I never doubted his love. He showed me in so many ways. His greatest gift to me, however, was his deep love for my mother. He worshiped the ground she walked on and I will never forget that.[1] So when I pray, "Our Father," it is pretty easy for me. I know that God was reflected in my dad, but He is so much more.

There is much that Jesus revealed about God as Father in the Sermon on the Kingdom Road. He is the Father who cares for the sparrows of the air and the lilies of the field. He cares when we worry, and He cares when we don't love as we should. He knows what we need, when we need it, and He is a Father who wants us to ask, to seek, and to knock. But one thing that strikes me about my Father in heaven, He is a God who wants to be called by a special name.

If you have been married for any length of time, you know that calling your spouse by his or her name is actually awkward. You have long since dropped the Margaret Alice in favor of "Shug," "Hon," or in my case "Ziggy."

111

And we all know it is in times of these greatest familiarities that we communicate the best. God, above all, knows that. So He wants us to call on Him with an affectionate name – "Father." When we really look to God as Father, communication is at its best. And this is not a stiff title – not one to be said with a long sad face, but a title of love and affection. Yes, we should be in awe of God, but no, we should not shun Him by our very act of prayer.

He is our Father in heaven. Heaven is a place, but we learn from early childhood that God is everywhere. So if God is everywhere, and heaven is where God dwells, then in my algebraic genius, I calculate that heaven must be everywhere too. It is a short trip for us in prayer to go from earth to heaven. It is as close as our noses. It is only a dimension away. So the journey there should not be hard at all. Just focus on the Father, keep your mind off the world and it won't be long until you are there in His Presence. You will know it the moment you enter in. You may enter with tears, or sometimes even laughter. But always, you will know when you are there. Maybe at first, a little music might help, or a sermon or a psalm or two, but when focused on God, you cannot help but get to heaven, if only fleetingly.

Praying to our Father in heaven can be the greatest joy. But dads, be a good dad, reflecting your heavenly Father the best you know how, so that you will not hinder your sons and daughters as they try to see God in their lives and prayers.

Holy Ground
"This then is how you should pray . . .
hallowed be Your name." (Matt. 6:9)

I will never forget the tears in Daddy's eyes when he proudly went to the bank to pledge his $500. The donation was to build a hospital in our home town. Oh, we had a hospital, but it was old, antiquated, and unable to meet the modern demands of medicine. His tears, however, were not tears of pride, but tears of rejection. The banker – the one in charge of the fund-raising – always took a personal delight in cutting my father down. This day would be no exception. As Daddy proudly signed his pledge card, the banker told him he had no business pledging income when he owed the bank money. Like I said, I will never forget that day. My dad was dishonored. No children, who deeply love their parents, ever want to see them dishonored.

This is a very practical lesson we must not forget. What child would ever want his or her parent dishonored? Have you ever heard little boys on the playgrounds of school telling of the heroics of their fathers? It is a natural instinct to exalt the ones we love. Because we love them, we want others to see their value. The problem with our earthly parents is that they have flaws. They have sinned; made dumb mistakes; and let's face it, they may not be winners in earthly terms. But our Father in heaven has never sinned; makes the wisest of the wise look foolish; and has never been defeated. He is all goodness, mercy, and power wrapped into a magnificent, beautiful, and awesome Being who is fully worthy of our praise.

Some people are confused in the Lord's Prayer, how Jesus could shift from the deep intimacy expressed in "Our Father," to the awe-filled statement of "hallowed be Your name." It seems that the two are at opposite ends of the relational spectrum. It is at one moment snuggling up to the Mighty One of the Universe as a small child snuggles in the safety and security of his or her father's arms, and the next being told to bow down before the King as a pauper in rags of unworthiness. Yet nothing could be farther from Jesus' teaching.

Let's take a look at the "burning bush." The bush was a very inviting sight. It drew Moses to itself. Of course, it did because God was within the bush. Yet, when Moses drew near, God told him to take off his sandals because he was on holy ground. That is similar to the opening of the Lord's

Prayer. God draws us into an intimate relationship with Himself. He is our Father in heaven. And we should come as a small child to his or her daddy. Yet, we must never forget who it is who is calling us. He is the Holy God. And whenever we are in His presence, we are on holy ground.

Isn't it awesome that this God draws us to Himself, that He desires a relationship with us? And doesn't it make sense that if I, as a small boy, was so angry and hurt at the banker for rejecting my dad's effort at community support and civic responsibility, that if anyone would say anything derogatory about my Father in heaven who created me, who has sustained me all the days of my life,; and who even died that I might live, that I would be crushed to the core.

God invites us onto Holy Ground, but we come there as His children. And as His children, we should wish for nothing more than for our Father's name to be hallowed, wherever and whenever it is used. Oh, that we could fear the fear of Oswald Chambers. I don't remember the source, but he wrote something like, "Our greatest fear in life should be that somewhere, sometime, somehow, someway, God's name will not be hallowed today."

Your Kingdom Come

> *"This then is how you should pray: . . .*
> *Your kingdom come. . ."* (Matt. 6:10)

Have you ever heard the old adage, "Be careful what you pray for, you just might get it?" Maybe more frightening is, "Be careful what you pray for young, you might get it old." Both adages, frankly, have kept me from prayer a lot of times as a young man, and have equally driven me to much thoughtfulness in my prayer life as I have grown older. I find that I am very fearful of what I pray for, simply because I most generally am too short-sighted to pray for what I really want or need most. It is a frightening thing, to look back upon my life and realize that if God had granted many things I had prayed for, I would be in a "world of hurt" right now.

Yet, there is no prayer that any of us pray that we give less thought to the consequences, than the simple piece of a verse, ". . . Thy kingdom come. . ." If God would answer that in its fullness, those three words would catapult us all into a far deeper reality than most of us ever want to venture here on this earth. I write and think a lot about the kingdom of God, primarily because I understand it so little. Therefore, I write and speak only as my most recent revelations have taken me. As I continue on in my examination of the Lord's Prayer, let me give you yet one more recent reflection on the "kingdom."

I said in the introduction that a kingdom is a place where a king reigns. So the kingdom of God must necessarily be where God reigns. Therefore, when I pray, ". . . Your kingdom come . . ." I must be praying, "God begin to reign now." Webster defines "reign," as "the exercise of a sovereign power." What, then, is the power that a sovereign power exercises? We would have to assume that the sovereign power will exercise that which is consistent with the sovereign staying "in power." For a nation, that would mean treason would be out. Presumably, so too, would such things as murder and moral decadence be forbidden, since they could undermine the purposes of the nation. Of course, as many nations as there are, it would be difficult to catalog the things for which they rule either for or against.

But sovereign above all nations is the Sovereign God. So, when God exercises His Sovereign Power, what would that look like? A few good places to begin looking are the Ten Commandments, the Sermon on the Mount, the Lord's Prayer, the Great Commands of Christ, and the Great Commission of Christ. So often these are cataloged as a list of "do's and don'ts," but I suspect that the revelation goes so much deeper. In fact, I believe those areas are (other than the Son Himself), the most important revelations of God. If that is true, then when we pray, ". . .Thy kingdom come,. . ." we are in essence praying, "Lord, begin to set up those things (the Ten Commandments, etc.) in our culture and in our hearts."

This brings up the trickiest part of the kingdom. What do we believe about those things (Ten Commandments, etc.)? Do we believe that God is serious about "loving Him with all our hearts, souls, minds, and strengths," and "loving one another as Christ loves us? Do we believe that He is serious about "going to the ends of the earth, beginning where we live, and making disciples (apprentices, learners, students) of all people (whether they look like us or not) and teaching them (training them) to obey all Jesus taught? I am convinced that if the Sovereign God reigned in our hearts and in our churches, that is what our community of faith would look like – loving God, loving one another, telling about Him, and demonstrating Him to everyone we see.

So when we pray (every Sunday as many churches do), ". . . Thy kingdom come . . ." we must be sure we want it, for we just might get it.

Let Me Do It

"This then is how you should pray . . .thy will be done on earth as it is in heaven." (Matt. 6:10b)

I guess I went through my child raising years a totally blind person. It all went so fast that I fear I missed it all. But by the time my grandchildren came along, I became more observant. All that is to say, I am learning a great deal about human nature from observing my seven grandchildren. A case in point. Marshall, my oldest grandson, is fascinated by computers and video games. But when he was small, when I would try to teach him how to play video games, he would yank the controls from my hands and say, "Let Marshall do it." Thus he was left on his own. Had he been able to sit and take instructions, he would have learned far quicker. (I now am a poor amateur on the games compared to him.) But the point is, his little self-will refused the one who could help the most.

Our will, our determination to do things our way, is generally the last surrender of our lives. A strong self-will has its place in worldly thinking. A strong- willed person is generally an over-comer. He or she cannot be held down by failure and rejection. They rise above their circumstances. On the other hand, prisons are full to overflowing with strong-willed men and women. The difference between successful self-willed people and criminal self-willed people is not just a matter of choices they make, but to what or to whom they align their wills with. You see, we all have a tendency, from the most independent to the most surrendered person, to align our wills with something. We can align our wills with good things, or we can align them with bad things. And ultimately the outcome of our lives is based on where we align our wills.

For Jesus, however, aligning our wills is never enough. He wants us to surrender our wills. There is a big difference. A person who is "good" in the world's eyes may not have surrendered to Jesus' will. And without that surrender, Jesus' will cannot be done. In other words, that "good person" is merely doing their own will, to the best of their human understanding. And that is never good enough for Jesus. He made sure every morning that He surrendered His life to the Father and did only as the Father willed. So when we pray, ". . . Your will be done," we are praying, "Lord, take my will and make it yours."

This is the last surrender of the human life. We may be willing to listen to God, we may be willing to study about God; we may even be willing to align our will with His. But to surrender my right to myself is the very last act of human surrender. Yet, that is precisely what we are praying for when we repeat the Lord's Prayer. Because, you see, unless my will is surrendered to God, then His will is effectively barred from my world and even to those with who I am in contact.

Why would Jesus ask us to totally give up our wills? That seems to run counter to our very creation. But you see, it all depends on our definition of why we were created. The classic orthodox Christian confession is that our purpose of creation is to "glorify God and enjoy His presence forever." And God cannot be glorified outside of His will.

What Jesus wants for each of us is to find the ultimate meaning for which we were created. That is encapsulated in: Love God with all your heart, soul, mind, and strength; and love one another as Christ loves us. We were created for Him, and thus we cannot find Him outside of His will. He will allow us to do things our way, but unless His will be done, we will never find the ultimate meaning and fulfillment in life.

Chapter 8

Looking Inward

❖

*"Give us today our daily bread. Forgive us our debts,
as we also have forgiven our debtors.
Lead us not into temptation, but deliver us from the evil
one. For if you forgive men when they sin against you,
your heavenly Father will also forgive you. But, if you
do not forgive men their sins, your Father will not forgive
your sins."* (Matthew 6:11-15)

Jesus began the Lord's Prayer in the same manner He began the Ten Commandments and the Beatitudes – with a focus on God. And that is how all things must begin. God is our purpose and our being. So we ask that He be exalted, sovereign, and willful. Then we ask Him for His person to dwell richly within us. The last three petitions bear that out.

Give Me
*"This then is how you should pray . . . Give us today,
our daily bread . . ."* (Matt. 6:11)

You know what I miss most about growing up - the kitchen table. Before the days of television, the kitchen table was the focus of the family. We gathered around the table not less than two times every day. Eating out was rare and reserved for an occasional Sunday. Mainly cafes were for hotel guests, travelers, and feeding the workforce for breakfast and lunch. Only in the big cities were there *restaurants* where people dined out at night. Certainly, except for a few truckers' cafes, there were not many places to eat. That made the kitchen table the center of the family. The table was a time of feeding, communication, and sharing with one another. Even times when we were not eating, we still gathered at that old round table.

Jesus loved the kitchen table as well. Some called Him a glutton, a claim He Himself repeated. Many of the parables He told were centered around the table – banquets, feasts, and the like. In fact, His very first request of the disciples after the resurrection was to give Him something to eat. Suffice it to say that food and the table were important to Jesus. He loved to eat, and He loved to talk about eating. Part of that was cultural. Much has been written and spoken about the Jewish table laws. Culturally, it was an essential.

But there was something else that was important to Jesus about eating. He is our Creator, and He constructed us to need food. It is part of the very process of life. Yet, Jesus wants us to put food in its proper perspective. He said, "Give us today, our daily bread." Actually, in the Lord's Prayer, even the entire Sermon on the Kingdom Road, Jesus is merely taking the Scripture that He had inspired and putting it in terms that He intended in the first place. This portion of the prayer is no exception. Here food (and indeed all material needs) are placed in their proper perspective.

Prov. 30:8-9 puts it this way: "... Give me neither poverty nor riches, but give me only my daily bread. Otherwise, I may have too much and disown you and say, 'Who is the Lord?' Or I may become poor and steal, and so dishonor the name of my God." This is so important to understand. Thus far in the Lord's Prayer, it is all about God. We are to pray for His name (hallowed be Your name); His kingdom (Your kingdom come); and His will (Your will be done on earth as it is in heaven). So often, well-meaning and highly competent scholars take the last three petitions to mean that after we pray for God's name, God kingdom, and God's will, then we are released to pray for our own needs. But I humbly object. I believe that the last three petitions of the prayer are still God-centered, and that our prayer is that Jesus Christ will be glorified in us. As you can see from the context of the Proverbs Scripture that Jesus is quoting, He is praying that God be glorified even in the food we eat. Paul, puts it another way. He said in 1 Cor. 10:31: "Whatever you eat, whatever you drink, whatever you do, do for the glory of God." Therefore, even our eating habits should be a matter of prayer. The issue goes even deeper than that, however. Our eating is for the glory of God.

What Jesus came to teach us is that God and His glory must penetrate every aspect of our lives. We are kingdom people. As kingdom people, we are far more than just physical bodies. More importantly, we are spiritual people. That part is eternal. We are here on assignment, and as such we must serve the King with our lives. Therefore, in the final analysis it's all about God. We honor His name, we yearn for His kingdom to come, we pray for His will to be done, and we surrender our bodies to Him – asking Him to give Himself glory by the way we eat, drink, and live in this material world. Thus while glorifying God with our physical beings; we grow in spirit and in truth. And the joy in that is that there, and there alone, we will find meaning and purpose in life.

Big Red Dogs and Porcupines (Forgive Me)
"This then is how you should pray . . . forgive us our debts as we forgive our debtors." (Matt. 6:12)

Another way we glorify God is by our forgiveness. Put negatively, there are few ways humans bring greater dishonor to God than through our unforgiveness. Unforgiveness causes our lives to get cold, stony, and unlovable. But seldom does unforgiveness do damage to the object of our bitterness. Take Burgundy for example.

Burgundy was the most beautiful of dogs. She was a dream come true for me. I had always fantasized having a big river- rock fireplace, a hunter green plaid rug on a hard wood floor, and a maroon leather chair. In my fantasy, I would puff on an aromatic pipe (I don't smoke, but thoughts of a pipe conjure up sweet memories of my grandfather), read my Bible under a dim light, and stroke the fur of my big Irish Setter. One day I was describing this dream to a man, and he perked up with a look of "hurry and finish your story, I have something to tell you." When I was finished talking, he told me of a man he knew who had a young female Irish Setter pup, and he wanted to give her a good home.

So Burgundy landed on a ranch in Southern Colorado – the perfect environment for her long-legged beauty and antelope-like speed. In the evenings, when the work was done, Margaret and I would sit on the porch of our house, which overlooked a 10,000 acre valley below. And Burgundy would run – she would run after rabbits, she would run after deer, and she would run after the elk herds which would from time to time try to take her on. It was incredible to watch her overtake a snowshoe rabbit in a few fluid strides. But there was one creature, although no match for her speed, that always won the races with her – the porcupine. When Burgundy encountered her first one, the results were disastrous. Being the conqueror of everything she took on, the "furry" little creature would be no match for her. So she bit it.

Puppy tears and loud shrieks filled our Bronco as we traveled 40 miles to the nearest veterinarian's. Burgundy had to be sedated to take out all the quills imbedded in her tongue and in the roof of her mouth. After about 30 minutes of surgery, I asked the vet if the trauma of the experience would prevent her from biting another one. The vet told us that she would either choose to fear porcupines and give them wide berth, or she would hate them. Burgundy chose the latter.

From then on, every few weeks, we found ourselves extracting quills from her nose. But one day, in her desire for conquest, Burgundy rolled on a dead carcass. No longer were the quills stuck in her nose. This time they were imbedded in her side. Again, I pulled quills, getting every one I could see. There was no change for a while. Hunting season was arriving. This time of year took me into the high country, setting up camps and preparing for the onslaught of hunters. One evening, two days before the season began, I arrived back at the ranch, dirty and smelly from a few days living with the horses. After my shower, I heard a knock on my door. When I opened the door, there sat Burgundy. She had a wild look in her eyes, as foam drooled from her mouth. After being sure she was not rabid, I reached down and picked her up. There in my arms, she breathed her last breath.

I took her into town to find out what could have possibly killed her. The vet did an autopsy and when he opened her up, he found her lungs were totally collapsed. You guessed it; they were full of porcupine quills. The dying blow came from one through the heart. You see, a porcupine quill is designed to travel inward. Once it penetrates its victim, the mechanism that keeps the quill firmly attached in the victim, is the same mechanism that causes it to continue to travel inward. Every quill I had missed when Burgundy had rolled on that porcupine had made its destructive way into the entrails of my beautiful dog.

We are all like Burgundy. And unforgiveness is like a porcupine quill. It firmly attaches itself to the person and travels inward until it kills. When we are harmed by another person, we have a choice. We can either forgive that person, or we can choose to hate them. And the spiritual result of that choice is the same as my dog's physical choice. The choice is a matter of life and death.

The Kingdom of God is within us. Like every part of the Lord's Prayer, this petition of forgiveness is rooted in glorifying God. Even the way we treat those who offend us spiritually, emotionally, or physically. Our forgiveness of others is a matter of giving up one of our deepest inclinations. And this must be for the glory of God. Granted, Burgundy was just a dog. And maybe she did not have a soul, so that forgiveness really didn't make but a few years' difference. If she had no soul, then her inclinations to sin or not sin were merely that – inclinations. But what about our inclinations? When someone harms us, how are we inclined to treat him or her? Some will say it depends upon on the gravity of the offense. I would say to them, I doubt if any sin against us is grave in relation to the sins we have committed against God. So then I ask again, what are our inclinations when someone sins against us? That may very well be one of the most eternally important questions we can ever answer.

When we bite the porcupine, we have a choice. We can either choose hatred and revenge or we can choose forgiveness. Jesus has given us that gift, but that gift came at a very high cost – His life. Just as with my beautiful Irish Setter, the choice is a matter of spiritual life or death. The hardness of an unforgiving heart will block the power that God has granted to every one who receives Jesus, but the heart softened by a forgiving spirit leads to an ever-increasing ability to glorify Him.

Deliver Us from Evil

"This then is how you should pray . . .
lead us not into temptation,
but deliver us from evil. . ." (Matt. 6:13)

Evil wears many different faces. Evil wears the face of an abortionist who is chasing the almighty dollar and evil is in the action of the anti-abortionist who kills him. Evil wears the face of those who promote homosexual behavior, and evil wears the face of the pastor who holds up the sign, "God hates fags." Evil wears the face of the adulterer who kills his spouse to collect on her wealth, and evil wears the face of the spouse whose abusive behavior drives his spouse into the arms of another. Evil wears the face of the corporate executive who willingly abuses his or her employees to fill their own pocket, and evil wears the face of the employee who steals from his or her boss. Evil wears the face of family feuds, and evil wears the face of the one who puts inheritance and property above family. Evil wears the face of unforgiveness, and evil wears the face of bitterness. Evil wears the face of Saddam Hussein, and evil wears the face of the church that persecutes its people. Evil has many faces, but maybe the most evil face of all is the evil that lurks in my own heart.

Sadly, Jesus said evil did indeed lurk in the core of the human condition. And to live a life glorifying to God, we must be able to root out that evil and replace it with godliness. Each one of us is only a decision away – sometimes the click of the mouse on our computers away – from the most destructive kinds of evil. Every morning when we get up, a world full of choices lie in front of us. With each one, we either satisfy the sinful nature, or we please the Spirit of God. By those decisions we can honor God or we can bring Him much dishonor. Isn't it so beautifully consistent that every decision and choice in life we make, ultimately boils down to that one issue? Do we live for ourselves, or do we live for the glory of God? When we understand that, we can fully come to terms with this last petition of the Lord's Prayer.

Let me tell you of a vision or deep thought that came to me recently that bears witness to the importance of this. Paul wrote, "Those who live according to the sinful nature have their minds set on what that nature desires, but those who live in accordance with the Spirit have their minds set on what the Spirit desires." (Rom. 8:5). The vision I had was in my contemplation of this passage. It was a vision of three kingdoms, each running in parallel lines. The kingdom in the middle was earth, or the kingdom of this world. The one on top was the Kingdom of God. The one on bottom was the kingdom of Satan. Both the upper and lower kingdoms were self-propelled in that they traveled by themselves. The one in the middle, however, was powered by the energy that people drew from one or the other of the two. I will admit this is hard to describe in such a way for you to get that vision, but the teaching the Lord gave me in that vision is worth passing on to you.

First let's take a look at the journey on the Kingdom Road. That journey is empowered by Christ Himself. He is the driving force. As He moves, He moves in righteousness, goodness, peace, strength, and power. And the more we can tap into His presence on that road, the more power we have for our lives.

On the other hand, the bottom road is slick, oily, and wide. The journey is empowered by Satan through the tears, heartaches, and tragedies of God's people. As it moves forward, it sucks down God's children. It takes the life out of the middle road and renders it useless.

The middle road is the road that each of us walks on. Sometimes it moves fast, other times slowly, but at all times dangerously. It has no power of its own. In can only exist and move by the power of the other two roads. And no matter what, the fuel for the middle road comes from either the upper or the lower.

Maybe you already understood this, but it came as a surprise to me. We live on one plane, but we exist on that plane by the power we receive from one – and only one – of the other planes. Paul said we have two natures – the way of the flesh or the way of the Spirit. And we can tell those natures apart by checking to see which one pleases God. If the nature is unpleasing to Him, then we are drawing our strength from the wrong road. Paul wrote we either have our mind set on the things of the flesh or the things of the world. And wherever our minds are set, that will dictate our behavior. For example, Paul wrote in Galatians, ". . . The acts of the sinful nature are obvious: sexual immorality, impurity and debauchery, idolatry and witchcraft; hatred, discord, jealousy, fits of rage, selfish ambition, dissensions, factions and the like" (Gal. 5:19)." Ouch! Sometimes Paul needs to stick to preaching and quit meddling.

The other way is also easily identified. Paul wrote, "But the fruit of the Spirit is love, joy, peace, patience, kindness, goodness, faithfulness, gentleness and self-control" (Gal. 5:22). And when we possess those things in increasing number, we certainly are moving the center road in a more meaningful direction.

I'm not sure I made myself, or my vision clear, but here is my point. The more people live according to the Spirit, the more the earthly kingdom resembles the Kingdom of God. But the more people who live according to the lower kingdom, the more the earthly kingdom resembles the kingdom below. So if you don't like what is going on in the world around you, stop and see which kingdom you are serving – for the kingdom of earth will reflect the faith of those living thereon.

So then logically, the last area of our lives that could so easily bring dishonor to God is our lifestyles and tongues. So we pray, "Lord, don't let me go there." Be careful little feet where you go; be careful little hands what you do; be careful little tongue what you say. This little ditty of a bygone era sums it up. "But Lord, I can't avoid evil. I need Your help. I need Your help in seeking to say and do those things that bring You glory and honor, and not to say and do those things that taint Your reputation."

Things are so simple when put in God's perspective. The moment we dethrone God and put ourselves on the throne of our hearts, the Christian witness begins to die, and the face of evil rests mightily upon our face.

Summary

Throwing pineapples into the fire? Hardly. This prayer opens the door for a relationship with our God and our King. Jesus knew that. Ritual, maybe. But it is only ritual when we don't understand what God is teaching us in our prayers or when we take lightly its deepest meaning. May every prayer be for His glory.

Chapter 9

Seventy Times Seven

❦

"For if you forgive men when they sin against you, your heavenly Father will also forgive you. But if you do not forgive men their sins, your Father will not forgive you."
(Matt. 6:14-15)

Somehow we think maybe Jesus has said enough in the prayer about forgiveness. We get the point. Or do we? He thinks not. This is the only portion of the prayer which He places a divine exclamation point – a verily, verily; a repeat for emphasis. So He must mean that He does not want us to leave our rest stop until we get this important part of the journey – forgiving others.

If someone slights you, is your first inclination to forgive or to give back an eye for an eye? John Piper calls the inclination for retaliation our wiring, which causes us to "default" when harmed. He asked the questions, ". . . Do we lean toward mercy? Do we default to grace? Do we have a forgiving spirit?"[1] Those are essential questions for all of us "non-Irish Setters." And if our inclination is toward revenge, we must be busy about changing our hard wiring, because Jesus said, "For if you forgive men when they sin against you, your heavenly Father will also forgive you. But if you do not forgive men their sins, your Father will not forgive your sins" (Matt. 6:14).

He would later tell a parable emphasizing that point. Once there was a very wealthy king who decided it was time to settle accounts with his servants. One servant had managed to pile up an enormous debt – in today's value over $25 million dollars. Because the debt was insurmountable, the king ordered the man's property be seized and sold and that his wife and children be sold into slavery to pay just a small portion of that debt. The servant was horrified. He fell to his knees and begged for time to repay the debt. This was a ludicrous request since a master servant in those days could not be expected to make more than $1,000 per year. It would take thousands of lifetimes to make even a dent in the debt. Knowing the debt could never be paid; the king had mercy on the servant and forgave the entire debt.

When the servant left the king's presence, he encountered another servant who owed him $12. Feeling full of himself, he grabbed the man by the throat and began to choke him. The poor man begged for mercy and asked for time to repay. The master servant refused and had the man thrown into prison.

The king's other servants saw what had happened, and they immediately reported the incident to the king. The king was furious and called this unmerciful servant back into his presence. The king said, "I canceled $25 million in debt because you begged me. Shouldn't you have had mercy on your fellow servant?" Then in his wrath, the king turned the servant over to be tortured. And then in shocking conclusion to the parable, Jesus told His disciples, "This is how My heavenly Father will treat each of you unless you forgive your brother from your hearts" (Matt. 18:35).

So if Jesus takes unforgiveness so seriously – and I challenge He does since He gave His life so that God could forgive us – then I believe we must be equally serious about

130

our own hard wiring or inclination. Every Christian must be intentional, regardless of their inclinations, about developing a forgiving spirit. And this is very hard. How then is it accomplished? Let me give you three ways from the King.

First of all, I believe that real forgiveness, the kind that comes from the depth of the heart, is truly impossible without Jesus. Luke tells us that as Jesus looked down upon war-torn, hate-filled, ego-driven Jerusalem, He wept, and cried out, "If you [Jerusalem], even you, had only known on this day what would bring your peace [meaning Himself] . . ." Sadly, today, hourly, daily, weekly news is filled with death and destruction in this city, because true forgiveness and peace is attempted with treaties, negotiations, and bullets instead of with the Author of peace and forgiveness. Only the cross of Christ has the power to bring about the magnitude of forgiveness in order to make the Middle East a place of peace and serenity. That may be global, but the same principle applies in our own hearts.

Jesus makes a difference. I am stuck on that phrase. "Jesus makes a difference." I am stuck, because, it has dawned on me, Jesus really makes a difference – not Christianity, not Catholicism, not Protestantism, not Pentecostalism, not religion in any form – but *Jesus* makes a difference. He penetrates the nooks and crannies of the lives of those who are surrendered to Him. Nothing is the same after He enters our lives. And when our lives are radically changed, then, too, are the lives around us. In my ministry I have seen brokenness restored by no other force than Christ. Other forces can put on bandages, but only Jesus can restore. Broken marriages, broken families, broken lives, broken hearts, broken relationships, broken churches, and broken bodies, all find wholeness under His powerful influence.

There is no place where this applies more than in this matter of forgiveness. Christ is the author of human forgiveness. Let me repeat that. Christ is the author of human forgiveness. If you were a Jew, sitting on the mountaintop, listening to the Sermon on the Kingdom Road, you would have been shocked when Jesus said, "Forgive us our debts, as we forgive our debtors." It must have had a ring of heresy to the hearers. Only God can forgive, and then only through repentance. In all the Torah, in all the Psalms, in all the teachings of the prophets, not one word is written about one human forgiving another. (An exception might be the story of Joseph forgiving his brothers.) "We don't even have that right," they must have thought.

That is why I said, Jesus makes a difference. Only Jesus showed us the power of forgiveness. Only Jesus told us to use that power. Burgundy was barely two years old when she died – robbed of another ten or twelve years because of unforgiveness. But maybe she didn't have that power. We do! We have in our grasp the power to forgive each and every harm done to us; every ill that befalls us; every hurt that is inflicted upon us. Jesus has given us that power and He has told us to use it. So I repeat, if we do not have Christ dwelling in our hearts, we can never achieve the level of forgiveness that He requires of us.

Jesus was serious about forgiveness, because He fully understood the destructive power of unforgiveness. I join with the 300,000 or so pastors in our land who can be witness to the awful, relentless, and all consuming power that unforgiveness has on a person's life. We have all seen horrible brokenness inflicted – persons against persons; families against families; church members against church members; pastors against congregations, congregations against pastors, and nations against nations. Unforgiveness can result in war that kills thousands, even millions. But on an individual level, we have seen unforgiveness destroy the soul.

We all have bitten a porcupine. Someone has hurt us, harmed us, betrayed us, or forsaken us. Some of the truly misfortunate have had family members killed by another.

Others have had their loved ones ripped from their hearts. Still others have been victims of the most heinous violence. I will never minimize the horrendous hurt these things can inflict. But heart revenge is never the answer to healing. Healing can only begin when forgiveness is applied. Jesus has given us the gift of forgiveness, but *we must apply it.* It must be central to the way we begin to restore our own lives after the hurt has been inflicted.

Jesus also understood the gravity of the harm unforgiveness does and has done to our relationship with Him. Our sin cost Him His life. This is no trite saying. Go back and watch Mel Gibson's, *The Passion of the Christ.* And I am quite sure, in spite of the critics feigned insult at the violence, that Gibson's version was nowhere near the real punishment Christ received on our part. An expression that pastors hear often when we counsel on the act of forgiveness is, "But Pastor, you have no idea what that person did to me." And I always deep down want to ask, "Did they beat you until you couldn't stand, then place a crown of thorns on your head, spit on you, mock you, and then order your execution? Did they make a public spectacle of you; make you carry your instrument of execution through the capitol city? Did they drive spikes into your hands and feet and drop you into a six- foot deep socket, throwing all your bones out of joint? Did they let you die of suffocation and then thrust a spear into your heart to prove you were dead? If they did that much, then maybe you have some right to unforgiveness." That is what I truly want to say, and lately, I have been prone to say it.

But in order to be able to forgive, we must understand what it is. When Christ forgave you, He wiped your slate clean. All your sins are gone, and God remembers them no more (Jer. 31:34). It was a total cleansing. And Jesus said, "As I have done for you, you are to do for one another." Let me just add, I believe the Golden rule is now obsolete for Christians. We must adhere to a higher rule. We are to do for others as Christ has done for us (John 15:12). I call this the Platinum rule.

Wiping the slate clean for a Jew to a Nazi must have been harder than most people could imagine. We saw the difficulty of that reflected in the relentless pursuit of Nazi war criminals after World War II. Please don't get me wrong, all war criminals are subject to law and must be captured and punished. But when the motive for pursuit of such criminals is hatred, then the lives of those hating becomes gnarled, and hearts become encased in stone. We saw that in the more recent trials involving a renowned athlete. Someone brutally murdered the athlete's wife. He was the prime suspect. He was tried and acquitted. Whether he was guilty or not, only he and the Lord know for sure. However, the wife's parents and family were filled with such hate; they could not rest until the athlete was punished. The court battle moved from the criminal arena to the civil. There the family continued to pursue their vengeance. They won a healthy financial settlement. I suspect the victory, however, was most shallow. The man they hate still is free to play golf, enjoy vacations, and live a celebrity's life. They, on the other hand, are left with the bitterness that flows from unforgiveness.

Let me tell you what I believe a good definition of forgiveness is. I believe it means that I give up my right to harm another, based on what harm they did to me. Using this definition, healing can occur in a victim of any level of offense. Let me repeat, "I give up my right to harm another based on what harm they did to me." Let me tell you a story I count as a great tragedy. I was sitting in a doctoral class on crisis preaching and was shocked to hear the advice that two "crisis management" pastors, who were serving as consultants, gave on forgiveness. They advised, "Victims of violence must never be too quick to forgive. Forgiveness too soon will stunt the healing process." As the hackles on the back of my neck rose, I saw that many of my fellow students were crouching for an attack. Frankly, I don't know how the world counts the success of this team, but I can tell you that these so-called Christian pastors have stepped outside the Scripture, and claimed a better way. And I fear for the results on the lives of those they have touched. Because, you see, God has given us a tool for healing, and that tool is cleansing our slate of hatred so that our hearts can begin to heal.

I have dwelt long on this subject, but I see unforgiveness as the root of much of the problems in the Church and Christians today, impairing our journey on the Kingdom Road. We have even institutionalized unforgiveness as witnessed above. There is nothing, however, that brings less glory to God than Christians being unforgiving after what Christ has done for us. Our bitterness, unforgiveness, and hard-heartedness to others demonstrate that we have not yet fully received Christ into our hearts.

The question then arises, how far should we go with this forgiveness? Peter wanted to know that as well. One day he came to Jesus with a question. It was a question we have all had to ask at one time or another. "Lord, how many times must I forgive my brothers?" (Matt. 18:21). I don't know what prompted that question, but I can guess. Maybe Peter had been raised by an uncaring father. Perhaps, his brother was trying to get the lion's share of the inheritance. Perhaps a Roman soldier had confiscated one of his boats. Or maybe Zebedee had encroached on his fishing grounds. Whatever it was, Peter was reminded again and again of the offense. Once, twice, three times. Surely he didn't have to forgive such a grievance forever. Maybe he was getting close. So Peter answered his own question with another question. "Seven times?" That would impress Jesus, because the rabbis of the day only required three times. On the fourth time, it was legal under Jewish law to extract revenge. So seven times would impress Jesus. Peter would double the amount and add one for good measure. That would make seven, the number of perfection. Jesus was going to be so proud of him.

Can you imagine the blank look on Peter's face when Jesus said, "I tell you the truth, not seven times but 70 times seven." I am sure Peter felt overextended with seven times. Surely none of the other disciples would be so generous with their forgiveness. But Jesus wanted more. He wanted an eighth time, a 280th time, even 490 times. How in the world could he ever be expected to give so much forgiveness?

Jesus' message is clear. The journey requires a rest- stop – time to be refreshed for what lies ahead. In the midst of that rest -stop, He reminds us that rest requires being in relationship with our God. "Come to Me all who are weary and heavy laden and I will give you rest." And we cannot be in proper relationship with God when our hearts are set on revenge, vengeance, or unforgiveness. So, as we rest, we must let go of the baggage of unforgiveness so that we can be refreshed and renewed for the journey ahead.

Part IV

The Destination Life in the Kingdom

༈

Chapter 10

Two Masters

◈

"Do not store up for yourselves treasures on earth, where moth and rust destroy, and where thieves break in and steal. But store up for yourselves treasures in heaven, where moth and rust do not destroy, and where thieves do not break in and steal. For where your treasure is, there your heart will be also. The eye is the lamp of the body. If your eyes are good, your whole body will be full of light. But if your eyes are bad, your whole body will be full of darkness. If then the light within you is darkness, how great is that darkness! "No one can serve two masters. Either he will hate the one and love the other, or he will be devoted to the one and despise the other. You cannot serve both God and Money.
(Mt 6:19-24)

What is it that motivates you? What are your priorities in life? Are they athletics, school, material possessions, work, play, or is it Jesus Christ? How you answer that will make an eternity of difference. Certainly this is true when we think about our possessions.

Jack and Jenny were the envy of all their associates. Jack was a successful vice-president of a growing computer firm. It seems that every thing he touched turned to gold. His decisions were always right; his investments were always on target; and his luck never seemed to run out. Ever since the company hired him, his story was one promotion after another. Every award the company gave seemed to go to Jack. Everyone knew that he would be the next president of the firm, and that day was not too far away.

Jenny, too, was the envy of those around her. She was a full partner in one of the most prestigious law firms in the city. Her legal mind was the best in the firm. Already at 35 she received every major case that came along. Her striking beauty always won the juries over before she even opened her mouth. And when she did begin to speak, the whole courtroom would go silent.

Together, Jack and Jenny were the toast of the town. No social event was complete without these two in attendance. They were striking models of marriage and parenthood. They had two young sons, ten and twelve, who already were demonstrating to the schools that they were following in their parents' footsteps. They were popular, well behaved, and were both at the top of their class in school.

So the whole town was in shock when Jack and Jenny announced their departure from their respective careers. As caring parents, they were determined to make their boys well-rounded young men, who had a strong sense of family. They made the decision not to give up their precious years with these two boys by chasing their respective careers. There would be plenty of time for that after the boys graduated from high school.

They had been talking about this for several years – breaking loose and doing something special that the boys would never forget. Now was the time. They were both in good shape, young, and financially able to make it happen. They sold their $750,000 home and all their major possessions; cashed in their stocks and bonds; boned up on how to home school the boys; and announced their plans to set sail on an ocean voyage that would last two years. During this time they would travel down the coast of South America, then across to New Zealand and Australia, then to Southeast Asia, exploring many of the Indonesian Islands,; up to Japan, then Russia, from Russia to Alaska and back down the North American coast to their home city. During this time the boys would receive an education of a lifetime, the family would grow closer, and the world would see what was really important to this extraordinary family.

Jack and Jenny had spent a year planning the purchase of their yacht, studying navigational charts, and planning the provisions for the trip. Now the time to go was at hand. They said their farewells, loaded the boat, and prepared to set sail the following morning. They spent the night in the marina. At 9:00 o'clock the next morning their close friends planned a launching ceremony and bon voyage. This was going to be the most exciting day in this young family's life. But all their planning, hopes, and dreams came to a shattering close that night in the marina. Two men, armed to the hilt, pulled up beside the boat and boarded. The black masks betrayed their intentions. Jack became an object lesson for any who stood in their way. They hit him over the head with a blackjack and then slapped one of the boys to the floor. They then placed the entire family in a john boat and stole the yacht and all its provisions. The yacht and the pirates were never seen again. Miraculously, Jack, Jenny, and the boys all survived the ordeal, but every earthly possession sailed out of the marina that night without them.

Their dreams were shattered. It was more than the couple could cope with. Within one year, Jack and Jenny were divorced and the ideal family was dead. Jenny continued in her law practice, but Jack just couldn't seem to get it back together. The boys, made it through okay, but life was never the same again. One day an associate picked up the courage to ask Jenny what happened. She said, "We lost everything. Everything we had dreamed about was gone. It was just impossible to go on." Jenny was safe; her family was safe except for a few bumps and bruises; they had their health and their life ahead of them, but the family saw no reason to go on. All of their treasures were vested in the boat and the provisions of the boat, where the moths could eat, the hull could rust, and the thieves could steal it away. And the words of Jesus echo through our minds, "Where you store your treasures, there your heart will be also."

Jack and Jenny were motivated by the world and when their world was stolen, they saw no reason to go on. They looked to the world to bring them all their joy, but Jesus tells us to look up – look to the celestial realm where we will find the true meaning of life.

We are not only motivated by our treasures, we are also motivated by the things we see. Jesus tells us the eye is the lamp of the body. If the eye looks upon things that are pleasing to God, the whole body is illuminated; if however, they eye looks upon the darkness, the whole body becomes dark.

Ted's first encounter with pornography was in the high school gymnasium. Now in those days, pornography was hard to come by in this land. Even Playboy magazine's centerfold featured fully clad women in seductive poses. But in Europe, that was different. Ted's best friend Pete's father had just returned from a business trip in Europe. Europe was no longer shackled to the Victorian standards of America. As Pete was unpacking for his father, he found some hard-core pornography his father had brought back from his business trip. He snuck the magazine into his shirt and took it to school. There he would be the hit of all the boys in his group. Ted was one of the boys who saw those pictures in the magazine that day — and his life was forever changed. He begged Pete to let him take the magazine home. Pete said "no," but invited Ted over to his house, where they could look at the pictures together and get the magazine back before his father ever missed it.

That set Ted on a journey from which he never recovered. He would go to Pete's house as often as he could, but that was not enough. He then found a source for some of the black market pornography, which was becoming more readily available. American standards were beginning to relax, so underground pornography became even more graphic. Day by day he became more and more obsessed. Until finally, his fantasies had to be acted on. Ultimately, his fantasies led to the rape, torture, and murder of twenty-three young women. And the dark soul of Ted Bundy was executed on January 24, 1989.[1]

Jesus said, "But if your eyes are bad, your whole body will be filled with darkness. If then the light within you is darkness, how great is that darkness." What is it that motivates what our eyes look at? Jesus says to look up to the things that bring light into the body and soul. We are motivated by the things that we treasure; we are motivated by the things that we look at; and we are also motivated by whom we serve.

Georgia grew up in a devout Christian home. She could not remember a Sunday when she was not in church. Her parents were gentle people, but they had rules. Sunday was the Lord's Day, and on Sunday, they would serve Him only. So if she were allowed to go out on Sunday evening, it had to be to youth group. Georgia graduated from high school with a strong sense of Christian values, but frankly, she felt smothered by all this Christianity. She believed in Christ, but did not believe that Christ had to be the center of her life. When she went off to college, she began to slack off in her faith. First, she began to miss church on Sunday a few times a year, but by the time she graduated from college she hardly ever darkened the doorstep of the campus church.

In her senior year of college, Georgia met Mr. Right. He was right for her in every way. He was ambitious, had a high sense of values, and wanted all the things in life that she wanted. After graduation, Georgia and Bill were married in her hometown church. They started their careers and married life at the same time. They joined a local church in the city where their jobs had carried them. After five years, they started their family, and after ten years, they had their family in tact. They didn't attend church very often. They were just too busy with life. Bill's job demands took him away from town often. He learned that he could travel cheaper if he flew on Saturday, so he would spend many Sundays in motel rooms preparing for his Monday sales presentations. And when he was home on Sunday, he didn't want to waste his valuable day getting dressed up and going to church. And Georgia, never wanted to go to church alone. Church was a family thing, and besides, without Bill around, Sunday was really a restful day. And when he was around, she didn't want to spoil their family time by taking a half day for church. But as they grew away from their faith, they grew cold in the marriage. Then one day, as Bill was packing for his trip, Georgia dropped the bomb. "Bill, I don't love you any more. I want a divorce." Bill was devastated. The next morning, instead of being in a motel room preparing for a sales presentation, he was in church wondering what went wrong. After worship, he asked his pastor for an appointment.

At their meeting, the pastor asked the very rhetorical question, "Bill, are you and Georgia believers in Christ?" To which Bill quickly replied, "Of course we are. We both grew up in Christian homes." And the pastor said, "That's not what I asked, Bill. I want to know, are you Christians? Is Jesus Christ the most important thing in your marriage, your family, and in your life?" Bill responded, "Of course not. We have bills to pay, children to raise, school and athletic events to attend, and still have a little time for our marriage. In all that we come to church when we can. But we just don't have time for the kind of religion you advocate."

Bill and Georgia are like many modern couples. They claimed to be Christian, but they didn't have time for Jesus in their lives. He was just part of the long list of activities that dominated their daily existence. But when setting priorities, Jesus came in dead last. They were content to serve God on some Sundays and mammon the rest of the time, serve Him with their lips and mammon with their hearts. They served Christ in appearance, but mammon in reality. You see, mammon is anything or anyone who keeps us from following Christ. And to this modern compromise, Jesus said, "No one can serve two masters. Either he will hate the one and love the other, or he will be devoted to one and despise the other. You cannot serve both God and Money." Bill and Georgia served their lifestyle. They had no time to serve God, and now the family they were serving was gone. But Jesus said, "Look up." Look beyond the lies of the world. Look to the things that have eternal significance. And the God Who gave us life; Who arranged for our marriages; and Who gave us the ability for careers; will give us all we need for life. But if we look down to this world – its treasures, its darkness, and its masters – our rewards will be only what the world can offer.

Jesus is telling us, the Kingdom Road is a road that our marriages, our careers, our families, everything in our lives must be on. We must store our marriages in heaven, and Christ will make them whole; look to Him, and He will make our careers meaningful; serve Him with our families, and He will give us many rewards on this earth and the life to come. Look up to the things above, and He will give you the world for free.

Chapter 11

Beauty and the Beast

❧

"Therefore I tell you, do not worry about your life, what you will eat or drink; or about your body, what you will wear. Is not life more important than food, and the body more important than clothes? Look at the birds of the air; they do not sow or reap or store away in barns, and yet your heavenly Father feeds them. Are you not much more valuable than they? Who of you by worrying can add a single hour to his life? "And why do you worry about clothes? See how the lilies of the field grow. They do not labor or spin. Yet I tell you that not even Solomon in all his splendor was dressed like one of these. If that is how God clothes the grass of the field, which is here today and tomorrow is thrown into the fire, will he not much more clothe you, O you of little faith? So do not worry, saying, 'What shall we eat?' or 'What shall we drink?' or 'What shall we wear?' For the pagans run after all these things, and your heavenly Father knows that you need them.
(Matt. 6:25-30)

I was sitting in a lecture on "friendship evangelism" when I first saw this picture. It contained a beauty beyond any beauty I had ever seen. And I know beauty. I have lived most of my adult life in the Rocky Mountains. I have seen the velvet on the budding antlers of deer and elk. I have heard the majestic cry of elk in mating season. I have seen 400-foot waterfalls and the subtle rills of the small "brookie" streams. Beauty? You ought to see my wife, daughters, and granddaughters.

One evening, while returning a snowmobile from Flagg Ranch, on the South End of Yellowstone, to Mammoth on the north end, I saw beauty. There is a rare phenomenon in Yellowstone that I have not witnessed anywhere else on earth. It occurs on God-selected evenings, just about sunset. The sky, from the western horizon to the eastern the sky, turns a brilliant pink. It takes the breath away. Add to the beauty of this phenomenon a land covered with a blanket of white snow. The blue sky becomes pink, and the white snow absorbs the color. The whole world bursts with beauty. It explodes. But God was not finished with me yet. He added to the scene two bald eagles. Their blackness against the carnation sky would have been beautiful enough, but their heads took on the brilliance of their surroundings.

As I was saying, I was hauling this snow machine back to Mammoth. It was an end- of- season trip, and quite frankly I wasn't happy about it. Snowmobiling in Yellowstone is a wonderful treat. It unveils all sorts of beauty in majestic and subtle ways. But for the employees of that grand old park who must ride the roads every day, it becomes routine, monotonous, and by the end of the season, even painful. Trying to avoid the Old Faithful crowd, I traveled the east road around the lake, which had technically closed for the season. Everything was white. The lake was white, the exposed earth was white, and even the spindly lodge poles were flocked in white. And then, almost without warning, the sky, the landscape, the mountain tops, the lake, and yes, the heads of the eagles turned pink. I shut the machine down and basked in the beauty of the moment as I watched the eagles cavort against the purely western sky. I say all this to say, I understand beauty.

Now that I have wandered far off course, let me take you back to that beautiful picture I saw in that lecture. It was a pair of feet – feet gnarled by bunions, twisted by time, and cracked by lack of care. They were feet that had accumulated many miles upon this earth, and each mile was a mile of love. All you had to do to see God's plan for each of us human types was to gaze upon those feet. You see, they were the feet of Mother Teresa. Hers were feet that walked upon this earth in service to her God. What could be more beautiful? I can tell you that the crimson head of bald eagles, the bugle of an elk, the roar of a waterfall, or a 24-inch trout on the end of a six- pound test leader can never compare with the beauty of that picture.

Beauty? I understand beauty. It drives my soul. It is the driving force behind my wood carvings. Not that I think I am God, or even particularly good, but I love to see the grains of wood take on the life form of one of God's creatures. But do you know what I like most about beauty? It is the irrefutable argument against atheistic teachings. Think about it. If "survival of the fittest" were true, how would beauty have survived? In theories that point only to form and function, what earthly purpose would beauty serve? Why would the "no-god" care if there was beauty to make us pause and be refreshed? Beauty is the eternal proof of God. It points to Him and makes Him known. I join with Paul (Rom. 1:20) in saying that if a person can look upon beauty and not see God, they are without excuse.

I would like to argue that beauty has an opposite. It is not ugliness. It is not distortion and lies. The opposite of beauty is worry. In the Sermon on the Kingdom Road, Jesus makes that clear. He tells us that even the lilies of the field and the birds of the air are adorned by God's beauty. That's our sign not to worry. Worry and beauty cannot co-exist. When you look upon real beauty and if you open your heart to it, it washes away worry. The only way you can worry in the face of your sleeping child, is to not let the beauty of that moment sink deep into the core of your being. Worry comes from trying to protect what God has given – without God. I love beauty. It tells me every day, there is a God in heaven who cares about what my eyes see, what my ears hear, and what my mouth tastes. Thank you, God.

I am not naive. I see the world torn by terrorism, hatred, greed, and disasters – Satan's perversions. Satan loves nothing more than to pervert God's beauty. He gives us insurmountable problems, unmovable obstacles, and unbearable heartaches. And in all that he takes our eyes off beauty and places them squarely upon the things over which we have no control. There is where the beast comes in. Over that which we have no control, we worry.

From the period 1941-1945, over 250,000 Americans lost their lives in World War II. That is a staggering loss of life. But in that same length of time, over the last four years, over one million Americans have lost their lives to cardiovascular disease directly linked to stress and worry. Four times as many as died on the battlefield in the greatest war in world history. We Americans, the most blessed culture that the world has ever known, are the most anxious people on earth. Seventy-five percent of all the world's psychologists, mental, emotional, and spiritual health counselors, and psychiatrists are right here in this land. And they verify that the number one cause of the disturbances they treat is worry, and the resultant stress and anxiety. These are extraordinary statistics for a nation that claims to be 83 percent Christian – the very people whom Jesus told, "Don't worry."

Everyone suffers from some level of worry – whether it's dreading tomorrow's test or fearing a parent's reactions to bad grades. However, psychologists tell us that the disorders caused by today's anxieties are out of proportion to the situations faced. For Christians, worry not only robs us of our energy and optimism by which God wants us to live, it also violates a command of God. Jesus uses this word six times in six verses, which means He is very serious about the fact that worry is foolishness, because to a child of God, worry is irrational. Look at the beauty around you.

Jesus began this part of the Sermon on the Kingdom Road by saying, "Therefore." And it is in the context of that "therefore" that worry is irrational. Jesus has told us we should store up our treasures in heaven, not on earth. We should fix our eyes on eternal things, not on earthly things; and we should serve God with all our hearts, because we cannot serve both God and the world at the same time. Jesus is calling us to an unconditional commitment. And to those who make that commitment He says, "Don't worry." Let me put it simply; "The more God is a priority in our lives, the less we have to worry about things." Worry is the beast that clutches our lives, handicaps our actions, and chokes away our health.

So to eliminate selfish worry from our lives, we must first understand God's great beauty and provision for us. He said, "Therefore I tell you, do not worry about your life, what you will eat or drink; or about your body, what you will wear. Is not life more important than food, and the body more important than clothes? Look at the birds of the air; they do not sow or reap or store away in barns, and yet your heavenly Father feeds them. Are you not much more valuable than them? Who of you by worrying can add a single hour to his life?" (Matt. 6:25). If God has provided us with beauty to enjoy Him, life to know Him, and a body to serve Him, He will also provide the fuel (necessities of life) to make those things happen.

On this magnificent road to the Kingdom, Jesus inches us along. If God has given us beauty, life, and body isn't that sign enough how much God cares for us? Jesus said concerning the birds of the air, "Are you not much more valuable than they?" And concerning the grass of the field, if God dresses them greater than the splendor of Solomon, "If that is how God clothes the grass of the field, which is here today and tomorrow is thrown into the fire, will he not much more clothe you, O you of little faith?" Surely we are more valuable than they. We are the ones whom God created in His own image; we are the ones for whom He sent His only Begotten Son to die.

We cannot read Scripture without understanding the extraordinary care that God gives to us. To Noah, Abraham, Moses, and to the entire nation of Israel, we see God pouring out His daily care and concern. Jesus loved to gather the little children around Him. He loved to touch the beggars, the blind, and the lame. He was a Man of unlimited compassion, because He valued all God's children so deeply. It was out of this compassion that Luke tells us, He squared His jaw and resolutely set out for Jerusalem. He subjected His earthly life to unthinkable torture – only because He considers us gems of great value.

Worry is directly linked to whom we serve. When our hearts are set upon this world we must constantly worry about the moths that can eat, rust that can destroy, and thieves that can steal away our treasures. But if we have an unconditional commitment to God, worry is irrational. He has provided all we need. He has given us beauty to know Him and life to enjoy Him; He has died to preserve that life eternally; and all He asks is our hearts in return. Can it be that we are beauty in God's sight? Is the circle complete, from the beauty given to us, to the beauty we give back? How beautiful it must be when we conquer the beast of worry and demonstrate our faith in God. As we take it in, we give it back.

You see, therein lies the answer. Not my answer, Jesus' answer. He said, "Don't worry about your life, what you will wear, or even what you eat or drink." Give your life to God.

Surrender! Give up! Yield! Or as Jesus said, "Seek first the Kingdom and God's righteousness, and [life, clothes, food and drink] will be given to you." Let me paraphrase the Greek here. "Strive above all else for the reign and sovereign rule of God, and His upright judgment, and there will never be a need to worry about life, apparel, or sustenance." God will take care of those things.

Striving for God above all else carries with it a secret ingredient. It makes the things of God the most important things in our lives. And when that happens, coveting disappears from our lives. What we want in life is precisely what God wants to provide for us. What we eat or drink becomes a gift of God. Faith? Yes. But it is a faith that comes from making God the center of our lives, and all His beauty, His promises, His glory become our purpose.

Chapter 12

Logging

꧁❖꧂

"Do not judge, or you too will be judged. For in the same way you judge others, you will be judged, and with the measure you use, it will be measured to you. Why do you look at the speck of sawdust in your brother's eye and pay no attention to the plank in your own eye? How can you say to your brother, 'Let me take the speck out of your eye,' when all the time there is a plank in your own eye? You hypocrite, first take the plank out of your own eye, and then you will see clearly to remove the speck from your brother's eye." (Matt. 7:1-4)

W e didn't do logging in the National Parks. The primary reason was that it went against the grain of the mission statement "to protect and preserve for future generations." Sometimes the policy was very consequential. In 1988 over a million acres of Yellowstone National Park went up in smoke. Timber, lying dead on the forest floor for years, had lost its lifeblood and when the combination of drought and lightning picked its spot, the magnificent park became a raging inferno. Without arguing the wonderful idea of our National Parks, foresters have found many benefits to logging. Logging provides the nation with valuable lumber, restores the land for wildlife forage, and in some cases provides recreation benefits.

Maybe Yellowstone has a good reason for not logging, but for sojourners on the Kingdom Road logging is a very good idea. In fact, when Christians aren't in the logging business, infernos greater than the Yellowstone fire can happen. Take for instance when a television evangelist lashed out against the sins of the people. He needed to go logging. His own eyes were filled with a forest. He was trying to perform the delicate surgery of removing the specks from the people's eyes when a forest as vast as Yellowstone filled his own. I don't know about you, but when my eyes get worked on, I would just as soon the optometrist's eyes were unencumbered.

You see, a sojourner who is not a logger is in great danger of being a hypocrite, and I can tell you that if there is anything that makes Jesus mad it is hypocrisy. If you don't believe me just read Matt.23:1-36. He casts seven woes on those hypocrites who were blocking the Kingdom from those who would seek it fervently. And you don't want to be "woed" by God. You don't want to be woed because you believe you have the keys to the Kingdom and it's your way or the highway. You don't want to be woed because your religious traditions keep others from enjoying the Kingdom. You don't want to be woed because you think more of the law than you do of building beautiful relationships with Christ. You don't want to be woed because you tithe, chew out those who don't, and then fail to show mercy on others. You don't want to be woed because you have a hard heart toward others, and jealously guard your own position in the church. You don't want to be woed because you have a perfect attendance record at church and have no relationship with Jesus. And certainly you don't want to be woed because you participate in firing one preacher after another, because you refuse to be a logger. (Ref. seven woes of Matthew 26)

Sometimes the Gentle Savior is not so gentle. For those in the above categories He has the harshest of words. "Woe to you, teachers of the law and Pharisees, you hypocrites! . . . You snakes! You brood of vipers! How will you escape being condemned to hell?" (Matt. 25:23). As I said earlier, I don't know about you, but I would be scared to death if those words from my King were aimed at me. And that is precisely why Jesus told us to be loggers. "Why worry about a speck in your friend's eye when you have a log in your own? . . . Hypocrite! First get rid of the log from your own eye; then perhaps you will see well enough to deal with the speck in your friend's eye."

You see, a heart turned to Jesus Christ is a heart that yearns for everyone to know Him and aches to help others find the joy of a relationship with Him. Speck picking, or judging, is only for the pure in heart. And you will be amazed at how small the specks look in others' eyes when you begin to see how impure you are in your own heart. I suppose Jesus does give us permission to do some speck picking, but only when our hearts are pure (our eyes are clear) and since our hearts will never be pure, I guess we are called to be loggers and not speck pickers.

In fact, Jesus is so jealous that only He be the judge, He said that by the same standards we judge others we will be judged. There He goes again, just like with forgiveness. He is using our standards that we impose on others against us. Is that fair? It is – if we are to be Kingdom sojourners, Kingdom builders, and Kingdom dwellers. How sad it is when someone cannot see the beauty of the Kingdom because of the people who call themselves Christian. Whether we are Pharisees (legalists) or Sadducees (liberals), whenever our actions cause the Kingdom to be blocked from others, Jesus starts woe-ing.

The main reason Jesus wants us to do our logging is that He has a far grander vision for us than worrying about the speck in our brothers' and sisters' eyes.

Chapter 13

The Grand Vision

❧

"Ask and it will be given to you; seek and you will find;
knock and the door will be opened to you. For everyone
who asks receives; he who seeks finds; and to him who
knocks, the door will be opened.
"Which of you, if his son asks for bread,
will give him a stone?
Or if he asks for a fish, will give him a snake?
If you, then, though you are evil, know how to give good
gifts to your children, how much more will your Father in
heaven give good gifts to those who ask him!
So in everything, do to others what you would have them do
to you, for this sums up the Law and the Prophets.
(Matt. 7:7-12)

Have you seen the vision? It is a vision of boldness and clarity unlike anything you have ever seen before. It is the one you have heard others talk about, but you have never quite been able to focus on anything so majestic. After all, life just happens day by day. There is no time for visioning. You get up in the morning, dress for work, work, come home, do your chores, share a little family time, go to bed, only to repeat the cycle for tomorrow. Visions are for writers, preachers, and those so wealthy they don't have to work. "But for me," you think, "if I can just think far enough ahead to take a vacation, that will be vision enough."

If you see the vision, however, you will know it. Your life will never be the same again. It transforms your thoughts and your habits; it even transforms the way you look at the world around you. That's the problem with visions. They take us out of our comfort zones and place us, not where we see ourselves, but where God sees us. And comfort zones being what they are, then most probably the vision is not something we seek. So many people, afraid of what God might show them, decide to stay where they are – in the endless rut of waking up, getting ready for work, work, coming home, doing the chores, sharing a little family time, going to bed, and rising to repeat the cycle again. And as long as we are content in that rut, God will not show us the very purpose for which we are created. The good news is that God will make us hate our rut so badly, that we will begin to look for a better way. And if we are looking in the right place – asking, seeking, knocking – then God will show us the vision.

I confess, I have been in the rut. Maybe I was different from others in that I always detested its ruttiness. And the moment I found myself there, I (not God) would inflict change. I would pack up my family and move to the next adventure. And I did this for 25 years. Some called it restlessness. Others thought it was a character flaw. Maybe it was both. But on that fateful day, when I began asking, seeking, and knocking, God began to prepare me for the Grand Vision for my life.

The vision, if it is from God, looks decisively like the Kingdom of God. It is a vision of a God- centered world, with God- centered people, making a difference for love, righteousness, peace, joy, and a host of other things that dwell in that kingdom (Heb. 10:28). It is a vision that never includes things that bring heartache to world. And even if the vision entails personal sacrifice (even death), it will be so pleasing in your sight that you will never want to live outside of that vision.

Sometimes the vision is dramatic. Saul of Tarsus can testify to that. He was off on a journey doing non-kingdom stuff. Then whack! Jesus showed him the vision in the most dramatic of ways. And the vision was so overpowering, so real, that Jesus felt free to send a disciple named Ananias to show Saul all the things he must suffer for the Kingdom. And to Saul, the vision was so compelling that he spent years in preparation for his historic missionary journeys. Then when on those journeys, he found himself in constant danger – in danger in the cities, in danger in the country, in danger from bandits, in danger from his brothers, and in danger on the sea. He was beaten, stoned, and left for dead, and put in prison more times than most theologians dare to number. Yet, it was all joy to him – because he had seen the vision.

But let's face it. Not many people have had a "Damascus Road" experience. Seldom does Jesus knock us to the ground and open heaven to us in such vivid clarity that we can remain as steadfast as Saul in carrying out that vision. For most of us, Jesus just puts a little dissatisfaction in our lives. He makes the rut seem awfully rutty. He makes the routine seem awfully dull. He may even make our lifestyles seem a little bit dirty. For whatever way He nudges us to look away from the rut toward the vision, it is at that time we reach what Oswald Chambers calls the "Great Divide."[1] From atop the Great Divide we can either begin to ask, seek, and knock, or we can fall back into our rut of the endless cycle. Tragically, in that rut we will never find the beautiful and great purposes for which God designed us in the drawing boards of heaven, and carefully stitched us together in our mother's wombs. Our gene pool, for which God has taken painful care over thousands of years to develop, without the vision, becomes just another rutted human life.

There you have it – the grand vision or the perpetual rut. Which do we choose? If we choose the rut, we can sit back and relax and let the winds of time sweep us into a vague memory on the eternal landscape. If we choose the vision, however, we must be prepared for a lifetime on earth of asking, seeking, and knocking. And the end result will be the same as Paul's. We will reach a point in our lives when we will join him in saying, "To live is Christ, and to die is to gain." We will walk boldly into life on earth, and joyfully into eternal life with Christ. That is the grand vision.

The asking, seeking, and knocking is really another way of saying fervent prayer. In the Sermon on the Kingdom Road, Jesus had much to say about prayer. First, He told us that prayer was between us and our Father in heaven. It is not to be a pompous display of our abilities to assimilate beautiful words. Neither is it to be a show to draw attention to ourselves. Then Jesus gave us a model prayer, which we have come to know as the Lord's Prayer. So then, thus far in the Sermon on the Kingdom Road, Jesus talked about attitude in prayer and format of prayer. These are the rest stops of the journey. However, He also gives us prayers for sustenance while traveling. Now He draws our attention to persistence in prayer – prayer which catapults us out of the rut and into the Grand Vision.

I can only wish I could follow Paul's admonition, that I should have the "mind of Christ." For if I could, I could more easily wrap my mind around Christ's perfect thinking. Take for instance the beautiful way Jesus begins this whole teaching about persistence. He first gives us an awesome progression to our prayers. He said, "Ask and it will be given to you; seek and you will find; knock and the door will be opened to you. For everyone who asks receives; he who seeks finds; and to him who knocks, the door will be opened." Ask, seek, and knock – each delivered with an ascending sense of urgency. That is where the grand vision comes in. First, we simply ask God for a glimpse. And when we see a tiny glimpse, we know there is something far better than the rut. So we begin to seek. And when we come to that point, we are almost there. We begin to knock at first, and then pound on the doorway to the grand vision – the Kingdom of God. And when we do, Jesus Himself will open that door for us.

Jesus starts the progression of our prayer, by urging us to ask. Asking of God is as foreign to us today as it was to the disciples when Jesus first delivered this sermon. We don't want to intrude upon God's time. We fear our problems are too trivial to bother Him with. We feel cold in our relationship with our Father and, therefore, feel unworthy to ask. But asking is an essential component in our prayers. For example, Jesus said, "I tell you that if two of you on earth agree about anything you ask for, it will be done for you by my Father in heaven" (Matt. 18:19). Again He said, "If you believe, you will receive whatever you ask for in prayer" (.Matt. 21:22). Dutiful little brother James emphasizes, "You do not have, because you do not ask" (James 4:2). These texts demonstrate that God wants a relationship with us strong enough to whisk the fear of asking away. This relationship is to be based upon a trust that gives us permission to ask Him for the desires of our heart. And when our hearts desire Him, how gladly will He give us a glimpse.

You see, the reason Jesus commands us to ask, as some might interpret this text, has nothing to do with getting what we want like a spoiled child. Asking, means asking God to reveal a glimpse of the grand vision. Because until we see that vision, we will be stuck in the proverbial rut. Jesus wants us to get just a glimpse. He told several parables about that glimpse, but let me give you just one. "Again, the kingdom of heaven is like a merchant looking for fine pearls. When he found one of great value, he went away and sold everything he had and bought it" (Matt. 13:35).

That is the grand vision. The poor merchant, once he caught a glimpse, was never the same again. His life was no longer bound by the buying and selling of jewelry. He was bound by the overwhelming desire to acquire that which has no equal. Jesus wants us to get a glimpse, by building a relationship with the Father. For in a relationship with Him, God pours into us what He has always wanted for us. The question is not whether He is ready to give, but are we ready to receive. Take, for example, David's ponderings in the 23rd Psalm. In that psalm, David compares us with sheep. No creature loves the rut more than the sheep. If one walks into the sea, they all walk into the sea. If one lay down, they all lay down. If one panics, they all panic. I am not sure it is a compliment to be compared with these creatures. But David's point is well taken. We will wander over the bare hills (or in the ruts), but God wants us to lie down in the green pastures. We want to go with the crowds and the noise (the familiar), but God wants us to be beside the quiet waters. We will take any path that lay before us (ruts are deep), but God wants us to take the path of righteousness. So in prayer we are not so much begging God. The reality is we, in true prayer, are in the process of submitting to Him. We are to go to God in prayer, submitting ourselves in humility, admitting we cannot see the vision for ourselves. Asking God to take over is not in bad taste after all. It is the way He has chosen for us to express our need of Him and to display our humble dependence on Him.

Just as asking is turning our eyes from the rut toward the kingdom, seeking is the way we get to the doorstep. So Jesus tells us, "Seek and you will find." When Luke quoted this teaching of Jesus, he repeated a parable that Jesus told. There was a widowed woman who pounded on a judge's door at night until she achieved her goals. And the judge, who was unjust, gave her what she wanted just so he could get some rest. Jesus said, "If that is how a judge who is unjust acts, how much more will the Father in heaven act justly." From the prophet Jeremiah we learn a casual seeking is never enough. God want us to seek Him with all our hearts. He said, "You will seek Me and find Me, when you seek Me with all your heart."

I will never forget a story I once heard about Henry Kissinger, when he was Secretary of State. Whether it was apocryphal or not, I don't know. And to remember the source from such a long time past would be impossible. It just happens to be one of those stories I tucked away in my mind for future reference. Now is the time to use it. It seems that Dr. Kissinger had asked a young aide for a certain report. The youngster brought in the report, a smile on his face, fully confidant of his facts. After all, of all the aides, Dr. Kissinger had asked him for the report. Kissinger picked up the report, looked at the cover, thumbed loosely through the text, and tossed it back at the young man with the question, "Is this the best you can do?" Dejected the young man walked out. Sometime later he brought the revision back to the Secretary. This time Dr. Kissinger seemed to peruse only a single page and, again, threw it back in the author's face. The same question, "Is this the best you can do?" Almost ready to resign on the spot, the aide restrained himself and walked from the room. After a period of deep study, constant revision, and determined clarity the future ambassador brought the report back. This time the harried Secretary of State didn't even bother to open it. He simply uttered the same question: "Is this the best you can do?" To which the nervous youth said, "Yes, sir, it is the very best I can do." A smile came across Kissinger's face. He replied. "Good. I will read it now. I was not going to bother until it was your very best." Apocryphal or not, the message is clear; when we come to God in prayer, He so often sends us packing, again and again. Not because

He is playing with us, but because He is determined that we give our request the full thought it deserves. God is serious about His grand vision for our lives. I fear that often my heart is not into this kind of seeking. "You are a Big God, I am a busy boy, so go ahead and give me what I want, so I can get back to work." And I scamper off to my "busy" day and put God to work.

First, we get a glimpse of the vision and we ask God for it. But God in His wisdom does not give us lightly what cost Him so dearly. We must seek it. The seeking will take us to the very doorway of the grand vision called the Kingdom. There at the doorway, with sweaty palms, we must make the decision – do we knock or do we turn and run away?

Knocking is sometimes good for you. It gives you time to think something through. Between the first and second knock, maybe you have time to just turn and walk away. For example, if you knock on a young lady's door to ask her for a date, the heart starts pounding. Just maybe this is a signal to break and run. Or knocking on a door to offer an apology (praying deep down that the offended person won't be there) can be a brutal experience. Even knocking on doors of opportunity can be unsettling. On the first knock – no answer. Maybe that is an answer. You knock again – still no answer. Maybe you just need to give up. Just one more time – rap, rap, rap. You hear footsteps. And by the time opportunity opens the door, you have thought it through to the point that you can walk through it.

Sometimes knocking on God's door gives us time to think something through. Even though God has a grand vision for our lives, He has given us this pesky thing called "free will." You'll get no debates from me about "free will" versus "divine providence." If you ask me if I believe in either one or both, I will say yes. Back to the grand vision. Because God has a grand vision for our lives, He has invented this thing called "knocking on His door," to keep that vision in tact. While we are waiting outside the door, we are graced with the opportunity to think about what the knocking was all about in the first place. Why did I ask God for it? Is it really what I want? Will it be good for me? And maybe most important, is it consistent with God's grand vision for my life? Hmm! Those sound good, so we knock again. Still dead silence. More thinking time. By now we begin to settle in our minds the whys, the hows, and the ifs. If it is good for me, if it is necessary to stay on course for the grand vision, and if I really want or need what it is I am knocking for, we hear the footsteps of God.

For the one who has caught the glimpse of the vision and has asked God, and then has begun his or her journey of seeking, and then has found him- or herself at the doorway to the Kingdom and knocks incessantly, God Himself will open that door. And when He does, we must walk through. But that is the easiest step of all. Because you see, only those who do not desire God at all can resist the beauty of the face of our Lord and our Christ. He created us for Himself and as Augustine said; our hearts remain restless until we find Him. When we walk through that door, the things of earth will fade into obscurity.

Yearn for the glimpse that will catapult you from the rut. Don't resist the seeking. And when you stand at the doorway to God's purpose for your life, keep knocking until the vision is clear. And like the merchant, everything you have will be deemed unworthy. Only Christ is worthy to pursue, and only the Kingdom Road will take us there.

Chapter 14

Reciprocity

꒦꒷꒦

So in everything, do to others what you would have them do to you, for this sums up the Law and the Prophets.
(Matt 7:12)

Tiffany was only six years old and weighed only forty-eight pounds, when her older friend Lionel began to throw her around like a rag doll – inflicting more than thirty wounds, many of which were fatal.

Andy was the class geek — only fifteen years old and the brunt of jokes. He carried a loaded long barrel .22 pistol to school – two classmates lay dead, thirteen others wounded.

Kitty was brutally attacked as she returned to her apartment late one night. She screamed and shrieked as she fought for her life. She yelled until she was hoarse. She was beaten and abused. Thirty-eight people watched the half-hour episode from their windows with fascination. Not one person so much as walked over to the phone and called the police. Kitty died that night as thirty-eight people watched in silence.

Less dramatic, but equally shocking, was the ordeal of Eleanor. While shopping in the heart of busy Manhattan, she tripped and broke her leg. Dazed, anguished, and in shock, she called for help. Not for two minutes. Not for twenty minutes. She cried out for forty minutes as shoppers, business executives, students, and merchants walked around her,; stepped over her, and completely ignored her cries. After literally hundreds of people had passed by, a cab driver stopped and took her to the hospital.

There are basic laws of the universe. The tide rolls out and with certainty it will roll back in. And there is little we can do about it. We can build jetties, piers, and causeways, but eventually the tide will win out. There is a law of nature which dictates that which goes out will come back in. We send love out and we will get love back. We send compassion out and compassion will be returned. Always the going out and the coming back in. This is the great universal law of reciprocity. We are to get back into proportion of what we give. Yet something has gone awry with the great law of reciprocity. The basic laws of nature have been short circuited by our sin nature. Jesus understood the effects of sin and set out to establish a new law of human reciprocity. That is why He gave us the eternal teaching that we have come to know as the Golden Rule. "In everything, do to others what we would have them do to us" (Matt. 7:12). This command addresses the basic sin nature of humanity that causes stories like the ones of Tiffany, Lionel, Andy, Kitty and Eleanor.

All people of earth, not just Christians, have some rule of human reciprocity. The first such rule, I call the Lead Rule, which is the rule of the modern generation. This is the actual rule of how many people operate, which puts "me first." The Lead Rule is stated in different ways. "He who owns the gold, makes the rules." Some say in New York, the Rule is stated, "Do unto others before they do it unto you." And in Los Angeles, "Do unto others, and then split." But in a more serious vein, the rule says, "Do unto others as they do unto you – treat them as they treat you." In other words,

"Don't get mad, get even." The Lead Rule is the rule of flattery and manipulation. "Do unto others so that they will do unto you." Even George Bernard Shaw, the famous agnostic playwright, got into the act. "Do not do unto others as you would that they should do to you. Their tastes may not be the same." The Lead Rule has one common denominator – me. This "me first" attitude is the impact of the sin nature and goes against the grain of everything Jesus taught.

But in most world religions, there are teachings that counter-act this "me first" attitude. In fact, many of these teachings were already in place before Jesus delivered the Sermon on the Kingdom Road. These teachings, I call the Silver Rule. They elevated human behavior above the "me first" attitude, by helping us to understand the world from our own perspective. The Jewish teachings of Jesus day drew from Leviticus, "Do not seek revenge or bear a grudge against one of your people, but love your neighbor as yourself." The Jewish Talmud took this passage and wrote this rule, "What is hateful to you, do not do to your fellowman."[1]

Judaism was not the only religion in Jesus time. In fact, Confucius, the Chinese philosopher, had stated years before, "Surely it is the maxim of loving-kindness. Do not do to others that you do not want them to do to you." And Buddhism said, "Hurt not others in ways that you yourself would find hurtful." Actually I have found seven other such teachings. But notice there is one common denominator in such teachings – they are always stated in the negative. Keeping ourselves safe, we treat others accordingly.

When Jesus Christ came on the scene, He set out to change the focus of humanity. Where pagans think about me first; and even other world religions call for treating others well for our own good, Jesus changes our focus to what is right. The rule for human life must not be self-centeredness; nor should it be self-preservation as other religions taught. Our rule for living must be righteousness. That is the context in which we pray and the same context in which we judge others. That is the Golden Rule. *"Do unto others as you would have them do unto you."*

But there is something else that is a subtle but profound difference in the Golden Rule. All of the other rules anticipate this reciprocity. Jesus does not. He does not tell us to do to others *so that* they will return the favor. He states that our behavior towards others is dictated by how we would like to be treated, with no real thought of ever having the favor returned.

There was once a man sitting under a tree close to a river. He was engaged in his early morning practice of meditation, when he noticed a scorpion entrapped in large protruding roots of the tree. The river was rising, and it was obvious that the scorpion would soon be drowned. The man leaned over the river-bank and tried to release the scorpion. However, each time he reached out to help him, the scorpion would inject painful venom into his hand. Finally, the man got the scorpion to safety, but not until the man's hand was swollen beyond recognition.

An observer watched this entire episode for several minutes. When it was over, he asked the man, "Why did you work so hard when it was obvious that the scorpion was ungrateful, and it is the very nature of the scorpion to sting?" The man replied, "That may be, but it is my nature to save. I cannot change my nature because the scorpion cannot change his." This is the teaching of Jesus on human reciprocity.

You see the things we are to do have nothing to do with what people give us in return. What we are to do is for our relationship to our Father in heaven. Jesus taught that the measure of forgiveness that we give to others will be given unto us by our Father in heaven; so, too, will the measure of judgment we use for others be used for us. This is the essence of the teaching in Isaiah. As he was addressing ancient Israel, God said, you can spread out your hands in prayer, but I will hide my eyes from you, because what you do is evil. God hears our prayers when what we do is right – seeking justice, encouraging the oppressed, defending the fatherless, and pleading the case of the widows. A constant message of the prophets and our Lord Himself is, "When we seek to serve His people, He will give back that same measure to us."

If the Golden Rule were applied to the world around us, just think about what a wonderful world it would be. Our newspapers would not be about Tiffany and Lionel in Florida, nor Andy in San Diego. It would not be about Eleanor and Kitty in New York. The #1 movie would not have been R-rated for violence, nor the #1 music artist a promoter thereof. Hollywood and the entertainment industry would stop the vile language, sex, and violence in music, movies, and video games – because it would be right to do so. Businesses, utilities, and government would treat people ethically and with grace. The Golden Rule would reconcile the differences between labor and industry. But in reality, as with all of Jesus' teachings, implementation must begin close to home. The Golden Rule must begin in His disciples' hearts.

This wonderful little rule is well known among most people of all religions. It is as well known to Christians as anything Jesus taught, except maybe John 3:16. However, Jesus left this rule for all human relationships. For us Christians, before Jesus left to go and be with the Father, He left us with a far higher rule. I call it the Platinum Rule, the rule of the New Covenant. The Lead Rule says me first. The Silver Rule says treat others with me in mind. The Golden Rule states do what is right regardless of the consequences. But the Platinum Rule goes farther than anyone had ever gone before.

On the night He was betrayed, Jesus gathered His disciples in the Upper Room. John tells us that after He had received word from the Father that all authority in heaven and earth had been given to Him, He set about to demonstrate to His disciples the "full extent of His love." As we read those words, our minds go to the cross. But that is not what happened. Jesus rose from the table; took off His outer garments and wrapped a towel around His waist. Then He knelt down and washed His disciples' feet. Afterwards, He said, "Do you realize what I have done? As I have done for you, you must do to one another. For no servant is above his master." Therein lays the rule for Christian behavior – the Platinum Rule. We are to do for one another as Christ has done for us.

Christ came to teach us, to love us, to serve us, and to die for us, and that is to be our attitude toward our brothers and sisters. If Christians would apply this rule today, there would be no grumbling in the sanctuaries. Younger generations would love and respect the music and traditions of the older generations. Older generations would appreciate the differences of the worship styles preferred by the younger. Lovers of hymns would sing joyously the praise choruses and lovers of the contemporary would respect the traditional. And then we would carry this out across the thresholds of our churches into the world. And if we did, our marriages would be rich and meaningful once again. In a land that is 83% Christian, crime would go away. The cost of medicine and government services would diminish greatly because Christians would be serving their fellow Christians as Christ did for us. The list would go on ad infinitum – if only we would do unto others as Christ did for us.

The rules of human reciprocity should be as sure as the tide going out and the tide coming in, but our self-serving generation has tried to change the rules, and chaos has resulted. But even the rules of self-defense and self- protection pale in comparison to the rule that Christ left us with. "Do unto others, as I have done for you." That rule will escort in the Kingdom of God.

Chapter 15

Two Roads

❦

Enter through the narrow gate. For wide is the gate and broad is the road that leads to destruction, and many enter through it. But small is the gate and narrow the road that leads to life, and only a few find it. (Matt. 7:13-14)

I hate to brag about a place, because before you know it, others will go there too. Then it gets spoiled. Take, for instance, the Cold Spring area on the North Fork of the Paint Rock Creek above Hyattville, Wyoming. As you pull up to the precipice overlooking this beautiful valley, you begin to realize you are in a very special place. You get out of your 4-wheel drive vehicle, and stand on the edge of the cliff, and you know it. You are standing in God's presence, looking at His artist's hand at its finest. Wow! Your breath is taken away! You spend a few minutes taking in the grandeur. Then after a while, you begin to notice the specifics. You see the majesty of Cloud Peak hovering over the valley below. You see the waterfall as North Fork comes tumbling to its journey to the Gulf of Mexico. You see the lush meadows fed by the snowpack of winter. You see the Paint Rock, surrounded by its protective trees, merging with the North Fork to continue their journey together. And then you see it. A tiny road – two tracks really – only a trail. Ah, it is the road less traveled. Maybe the fishing is good. Maybe it is not quite so encumbered with the pressure of tourist fishermen. Maybe this is the place.

The road to the trail is narrow and steep. It is rocky and has won victory over many a transmission. It winds, it twists, and it goes very close to the edge. But I suspect that there are few places more beautiful than the Paint Rock Creek – at least to my eyes. Maybe the journey is worth it. Maybe that lunker trout still exists in the lower 48. Maybe I can get him. (He's hanging on my wall.) Whoops! I did it again. Look for pavement on the Paint Rock soon.

The tragedy of most places of the wonderful places in the Rocky Mountain West is that we have built roads to them. Broad and easy roads. The scenery is still good, but don't count on the fishing. The Bear Tooth Highway is a great example. Once it was a narrow road, but today, it is broad and wide. Any car can go on it. It is beautiful, but it is crowded. There are lots of people who enjoy the easy road. They can go on it, and they don't have to worry. There are even a few scary turns for excitement. And the trout? Don't bring a very big skillet. Paradise is wounded.

We have a choice of the roads we take. We can take the broad and easy roads. They are well paved and easy to maneuver on. Lots of folks take those roads. But don't expect to find the joy that you can find on the roads less traveled. Can't happen. Won't happen. Before I take the analogy too far however, I want to acknowledge that for physically challenged folks, I am really glad the Bear Tooth, Trail Ridge, and other fine Rocky Mountain highways exist. But you get my point. Life is full of choices. In fact, Scripture speaks a lot about choices.

Take the one on Mount Carmel that day. There was great excitement that day as the people gathered around Mount

Carmel. Two great enemies were matched up. Israel's popular king and the old runaway prophet who had brought a curse on the land were now about to do battle. On Ahab's side were 450 prophets of Baal and another 450 prophets of Asherah. On the other side, stood Elijah, alone except for his God. But before the contest began, Elijah cried out to the people, "How long will you waver between two opinions? If the Lord is God follow Him; but if Baal is God, follow him" (1 Kings 18:21).

These are the words that have echoed down through history. They are the words of choice. God from the very beginning has set apart a people for Himself, but He gives them a clear choice – follow Him or follow the world. This began in the Garden of Eden – the tree of life or the tree of the knowledge of good and evil. Moses delivered God's chosen people to the very gates of the Promised Land, and he told them, "Before you lies a choice. You can choose life and prosperity or you can choose death and destruction" (Deut. 30:15, author's paraphrase). Forty years later, after Joshua had been instrumental in conquering the Promised Land, he, too, stood before the people and gave them a choice. ". . . Choose this day whom you will serve. . . . As for me and my house we will serve the Lord" (Joshua 24:15).

These choices are images of the two roads that were laid out by our Lord Jesus, in the Sermon on the Kingdom Road. He said, "There are two roads, one is broad and gentle. The other is narrow and steep. The one road is down hill and many can walk side by side. Its destiny is total destruction. The other road is steep. Only one person at a time can walk upon it. And the destiny of that road is eternal life." Paul echoed those words when he wrote, "The wages of sin is death; but the gift of God is eternal life in Christ Jesus" (Rom. 6:23).

Let's take a more careful look at these pairs of choices that Jesus lays before us, because they may be the most important choices we will ever make, and trout fishing is incidental. First, Jesus said there are two gates. Guarding the entrance of the broad path is a very wide and inviting gate. There are no locks to keep people out – in fact, it is well decorated to invite people in. We can carry all the baggage we want through that gate. We don't have to leave anything behind. We can take our sin, our self-righteousness, and our pride. Maybe best of all we can take as many of our old friends as we want. But the other gate is narrow. You have to look for it to find it. In fact, this gate is very easy to miss – it is as narrow as the eye of a needle. To enter we must leave everything behind. We must unload our sin, our self-righteousness, and our covetousness. We must enter through this gate one person at a time.

But notice how Jesus began this passage. He said, "Enter through the narrow gate." In most Christian circles today, the gate is said to be wide open to anyone of any belief. And when this happens, it is much like a huge funnel. People come to Jesus with no thought of the sins of their lives. They just come for comfort and psychological needs, not for God and His Kingdom. So many people take these first steps into a wide gate. However, as they begin their journey, they soon discover the way becomes narrow. To continue down the road would mean lightening the load. And when many near the end, they find the Kingdom too restrictive. They have been induced with talk of healing, meaning, and peace of mind, and then suddenly they learn of sin and repentance, obedience, and discipleship. And rather than change their mind- sets they return to the wide open way.

But turn the funnel's cone around. Enter through the narrow gate. There is no admittance with baggage. We enter solely on the conditions laid down by Jesus. That means unloading our baggage through repentance, baptism, discipleship and obedience. Once inside, the person is astounded at how light the burdens, how wide the horizons. So when

Jesus said, "Come to Me all who are weary and heavy laden," the meaning is clear. Unload the baggage outside, and inside with a relationship with Him, the burdens are light. No one can be a follower of Christ, who has not first denied himself. (Have you ever let your bare feet hang down into a Rocky Mountain stream? Have you ever hooked a magnificent cutthroat trout on a four- pound test line? If you have, you know the narrow gate was worth lightening the load.)

Then there are the roads themselves. Jesus says there are two. One road is wide and easy, and it is on the other side of the wide gate. It will accommodate many people, all enjoying the spacious tours. There is plenty of room on this road for a diversity of ideas. You can believe anything on this road you want to believe. You don't have to believe in salvation through Christ alone – in fact, the teachers on this road laugh at such notions. On this road you can have lax morals and obedience. It is a road of tolerance and permission. There are no curbs, no boundaries of conduct or thought. Travelers on this road can "do it their way." On this road we find superficiality; self-love, and hypocrisy. You don't have to study; you don't have to practice. Remember the road is broad and easy.

The other road is the road less traveled. It is narrow and steep, and it has definite boundaries. Those boundaries are clearly marked by divine revelation. The relatively few pilgrims who walk on the narrow way are confined by what is right and what is true. This way is God's way. Poverty of spirit is not easy; turning the other cheek, walking the extra mile is never easy; prayer is not easy; righteousness is not easy; transformed, God-centered attitudes are not easily achieved. There is no room on this road for my opinions when they conflict with God's. There is no room on this road for my goals if they conflict with God's plan for my life. There is no room for relationships of which Christ would disapprove.

As I describe this road, there is a danger that it will be seen as dull and morbid – sort of misery now for pie in the sky later. But nothing could be further from the truth. On this road is the only real joy and freedom in life. There is no joy on earth that can match knowing God in Christ Jesus. There is a great liberty in forgiven sins and triumph over temptation. As God becomes the center of life, all life takes on a new and fascinating attraction as we catch glimpses of the kingdom to come.

In Rocky Mountain National Park, there is a beautiful high mountain lake. Many magnificent photos have been taken there. The first time visitor to Bear Lake knows immediately that they have seen this somewhere before, probably on some calendar. The pictures always portray this as a beautiful mountain wilderness, full of fresh smells and adventures. But when the first time visitor arrives he learns that the snapshots were taken with a massive parking lot behind the photographer. Totally surrounding the lake is an asphalt path with plenty of resting benches along the way. On a beautiful summer day, it is hard to tell the crowds from crowds on the Platt River Trail which runs through downtown Denver. The sojourners are the people who are too busy to explore the more narrow paths; too lazy to climb the steep paths; and too calloused to appreciate the pristine wilderness along the less traveled trails. And you can hear them making coarse jokes about those venturing into the wilderness. They call them deep breathers, tree huggers, nature freaks. But as you travel up the wilderness trails, the farther you go, the more pristine the beauty; the less people you will find; and the greater the chance to have an encounter with God.

And then Jesus tells us that each road has a final destination. You see neither the gate through which you enter nor the road that you take is of ultimate importance. What ultimately matters is *where* the road takes you. One road's destination is destruction and the other's is life. The road that leads to destruction is the wide road behind the big gate. The tragedy is that people become so enamored with the popularity and spaciousness of the pathway that they give little thought to its destination. And when they are confronted with its ultimate destination, they deny it; they argue they are no worse than the others on the same road; and in any event, God is a God of love and will not destroy anyone.

Nowhere in Scripture is this kind of optimism allowed. Jesus always insists that only the narrow way leads to life. Only the pathway that seems the most confining explodes in the end into a vitality, beauty, and joy of the Kingdom of God. But let me make it clear at this point; God has no interest in destroying anyone. He is the Creator, not the destroyer. And He created us for life, not death and destruction. That is why God detests the broad road. He knows it is a downhill slope to the destruction of everything that is good, lovely, and beautiful.

But ultimately God gave us the ability to choose. And there is an inescapable choice for each of us. It's either God's way or Satan's way. There is no other choice. There is no other way to life; there is no other way to avoid destruction than God's way. We cannot attain the Kingdom by worshiping nature, rocks, crystals, or our own desires. We cannot get there by some pious sentiment about the God of love. We cannot drift into salvation without decision and commitment. To enter life, we must submit to Christ, His principles, and His way. On this matter, Jesus is emphatic. He says we must enter through the narrow gate, and in John 10, Jesus tells us He is that gate. There is no other way; there is no other truth; there is no other way to life.

Chapter 16

Wolves, Buckthorns, and Thistles

✻

*Watch out for false prophets. They come to you in sheep's
clothing, but inwardly they are ferocious wolves. By their
fruit you will recognize them. Do people pick grapes from
thornbushes, or figs from thistles? Likewise every good tree
bears good fruit, but a bad tree bears bad fruit.
A good tree cannot bear bad fruit,
and a bad tree cannot bear good fruit.
Every tree that does not bear good fruit is
cut down and thrown into the fire.
Thus, by their fruit you will recognize them.* (Matt 7:15-20)

There were many in the city who thought it was impenetrable. Others denied that there was even an enemy
beyond its walls. After all, who could attack God's people?
Still others went about their daily lives, not giving it any
thought at all. But one prophet – Jeremiah – knew better. All
he really had to do was look outside the walls of Jerusalem.
Nebuchadnezzar had been camped out there for days. The
siege ramps were being built before their very eyes. It
was only a matter of days before God's people would be
captured, executed, and slaughtered. Day after day, Jeremiah

proclaimed God's word in the temple courts, begging the people to surrender before this came about. But his voice was silenced by the other prophets.

Scripture said, "[These prophets] treated the wounds of the people as though they were not serious." They said, "God is not that mean and your sin is not that serious and after all you are God's people – so do not worry – Jeremiah is a reactionary." And they reassured the people that the king would strike a peace with Nebuchadnezzar. "Peace, peace," they said, when peace was not a possibility. And within a few short weeks, all the king's family was destroyed, the people were slaughtered in the streets, and the prophets were executed. The few people who were left were taken into captivity and exiled to Babylon.

False prophets – wolves in the flock. Jesus knew His inspired word. His warnings were becoming not quite so user- friendly — two roads, two gates, two destinations; now, two teachings. As in the days of Jeremiah, we are told that our sins are not serious, there is no destruction, and real peace exists on this broad and spacious road. Jesus warned His disciples of this reality, and even today, we need to know that the church and our culture are filled with teachers who entice us to the broad path that will lead to our eternal damnation.

"Watch out for false prophets." In biblical times, a prophet was a person who spoke to the people from God. Jeremiah teaches us that a true prophet is a person who stands in the daily council of the Lord. In that council they hear His word and they proclaim it to the people — without error. We tend to think of prophecy as foretelling the future. And while that is part of the role of the prophet, it is only a small part. Down through the ages, God has used prophets to comfort, to warn, and to challenge the people. The main job is to speak directly to the people for God. In Jeremiah's day, there were men who claimed to be prophets, but they told the people what they wanted to hear. In Jesus day, the same thing was happening. And later, Paul told Timothy that the gathering of false prophets would be a sign of the end times. He said, "A time is coming when people will gather around them teachers who will tell them what their itching ears want to hear" (2 Tim. 4:3, author's paraphrase).

This is an important backdrop in understanding what Jesus meant when He said, "Watch out for false prophets." There will always be people, claiming to speak for God, who are indeed speaking on their own. Or worse yet, speaking on behalf of Satan, whether they know it or not. In the context of this passage, the false prophet is a preacher, a teacher, or someone in authority who claims they are speaking for God when they advocate the broad and easy way. Their job is to keep us away from the narrow way.

Now let me be quick to point out – Jesus is not here talking about cults. He is not talking about those who directly try to lure us away from our values. Disciples of Jesus are not very susceptible to an open invitation to sin. The false prophets are not likely to be preachers who advocate raw hedonism, anarchy, or forms of unbelief. The problem will lie with preachers who have all the outward trappings of a Christian. They may appear pious, prayerful, and they may even use all the right religious clichés; they may even be garbed in religious outfits. Satan himself cloaks himself as an angel of light. No, Jesus is saying that a false prophet is someone in our midst who does not advocate the narrow way; they say the gospel does not require decision, commitment, or discipleship. They leave out the hard parts of Christianity. They say, "All it requires is love." In other words, like the prophets in Jeremiah's day, they tell us that our sin is not all that serious; and that God is not really all that mad.

These false prophets are predators. Literally they prey upon God's flock, — God's people. Jesus said, "They come to you in sheep's clothing, but inwardly they are ferocious wolves." The very reason they come into the church is to seek out and destroy. God's people make ravenous wolves even hungrier. But they sneak in and prey on the weakest of the flock. They prey on those who are not sojourners on the Kingdom Road. They devour the uncaring, unloving, unforgiving, and undisciplined, who have become the weak sheep that are so tasty in the mouths of the ravenous appetites.

Careful examination of the Word of God can shine a great light on who these wolves are. They are the ones who lure the undisciplined into their traps. They speak of baptism without repentance, belief without commitment, membership without discipleship, grace without confession, and mercy without justice.[1] They lure the sheep into the traps of complacency, marginality, and nominality.

And you see, Jesus says this is nothing short of ferocious. It is ferocious or ravenous to lure God's people away from the very path that will save them, to walk in the way that requires little restriction of belief or behavior; to teach that there is no such thing as destruction. No wonder Jesus calls them ravenous or ferocious —— they are responsible for leading people to the very destruction they say does not exist. Satan has no greater joy today than the pulpits that claim he does not exist. Only in that belief, will our guards be let down, and the angel of light can become the roaring lion that devours.

There is a way to spot these wolves. Jesus shows us how. "By their fruits you will recognize them. Do people pick grapes from thorn bushes or figs from thistles? Likewise every good tree bears good fruit, but a bad tree bears bad fruit. A good tree cannot bear bad fruit, and a bad tree cannot bear good fruit. Every tree that does not bear good fruit is cut down and thrown into the fire. Thus by their fruits you will recognize them." In Israel there grows a bush known as a buckthorn bush whose fruit resembles a cluster of grapes. And there is a thistle, whose flower clusters and folds in such a way as it appears at a distance to be a fig. The point is clear. There may be a superficial resemblance between the true prophet and the false prophet. The false prophet may be dressed in the robes of Lutheran, Presbyterian, Methodist, or Catholic churches; they may have crosses draped around their necks; they may have degrees and pedigrees that run from Fort Worth to Chicago; from New York to Los Angeles; and they may even speak the right language of Christianity, but you can no more be sustained by the food of the false prophets than you can by the fruit of the thistle or the buckthorn bush.

Jesus said, **"By their fruits you will know them."** There are two tests or two fruits of the false prophet. The first fruit of false prophets is their character and conduct. They may appear pious and good on the outside, but given enough time their character will expose who they are. As surely as the wolf cannot stay in the midst of the flock without fulfilling his natural urges to eat sheep, neither can a false prophet follow always the narrow road of Jesus.

In a very large Southwest City there is a large denominational church in the downtown area. It once boasted over ten thousand members of the city's most respected and elite patrons. The pastor had become a legend. Dressed in his fine robes and religious attire, every Sunday he would proclaim a very permissive gospel. He would expound on the love of God and the freedom of Christians. He would rail against those who taught about the narrow way. He gave his flock permission for any kind of behavior they wanted. He had become a legend for church growth people.

One day, a friend of mine was trying to raise money for a Billy Graham Crusade, which was to be held in a sister city. He went to this pastor for commitment and financial assistance. After my friend's presentation, the pastor laughed at him and said, "I outgrew Billy Graham a long time ago." A few years ago, the whole state was shocked. This false prophet of the easy way was accused of seducing and having affairs with seven members of his congregation and numerous others in town. Although he plea bargained to lesser crimes – after over ten years of leading his flock down the very wide path – his character and conduct exposed him for the ferocious wolf that he was.

The second test of false prophets is what they teach. Do they conform to the words of Jesus, or are they filled with flowers and berries that at a distance appear real, but upon closer examination are deadly. Easy-ism or cross carrying is the major difference. There is a narrow gate, through which we must enter the narrow way that leads to life. Those who walk in that way find that while it is not easy to say no to the temptations of the world, they find that a much deeper joy comes in being a sojourner on the more difficult road – walking shoulder to shoulder with the King.

Chapter 17

Lord, Lord

꩜

*"Not everyone who says to me, 'Lord, Lord,' will enter the
kingdom of heaven, but only he who does the will of my
Father who is in heaven. Many will say to me on that day,
'Lord, Lord, did we not prophesy in your name, and in your
name drive out demons and perform many miracles?'
Then I will tell them plainly, 'I never knew you.
Away from me, you evildoers!'*
(Matt. 7:21-23)

My dad used to say, "You're talking just to hear your head rattle." I never quite understood the exact meaning, but I got the point. Be quiet! As I have grown older, I embrace those words. I meet a lot of people who talk just to hear their heads rattle. I remember Luke. He was retired and had little to do, but oh how he loved to do nothing in my study. He would come on his way to "coffee." His mission was to collect as much dirt as he could before going down to the local café with his buddies and share what he knew about the church. At first I thought he cared about the sick, but I soon got the hint. He would then drop back in after his morning "coffee" on some occasions and warn me, "A lot of

189

people are [upset, concerned, angry, disappointed]" at something I had done. "A lot of people" usually meant the ones he could stir up at the coffee house.

Most pastor's have a Luke or a Lily in their congregations. – people who put on the facade of a Christian, but are really more like those who never grace the doorsteps of a church, read a Bible, or say a heartfelt prayer. They cry "Lord, Lord," but in reality Jesus is anything but Lord of their lives. Jesus talked about those folks. He was talking about people who profess His name just to hear their heads rattle. These are like the false prophets, the wolves, and the destroyers of the flock. They put on the sheep's garb, but have destruction in their hearts.

Maybe these are the very ones who need the journey on the Kingdom Road the most, but sadly, it is these who are most likely to believe they are already there. Christianity has become practice not relationship; appearance not discipleship; and vocalization not action. Fearfully, it is these very ones who may hear, "Go away from Me, I never knew you." What Jesus warns us about is that we must be careful that what we say equals what we do. So if we call Him Lord, we best let Him be Lord.

I think it would be useful here to understand what it means for Jesus to be Lord. First of all, we must not mistake here what Jesus was calling Himself. The word "Lord" in the New Testament is the word, *kurios*. *Kurios*, the Greek word used in the Greek Old Testament (Septuagint) from which Jesus liberally quotes, means Yahweh, Jehovah – the only name that God calls Himself. So when Jesus said, "Not everyone who calls me 'Lord, Lord,'..." He is ascribing the name of God to Himself. This brings even more clarity to what He is saying. Literally in Greek, *kurios* means the one to whom another belongs, who decides their fate. If He is Lord, then we must understand that we belong to Him, and He alone will decide our fate.

I hear people pray, "Lord, help me to overcome this or that." But whether or not the Lord answers that prayer makes no difference in how that person lives. Ask any pastor their greatest frustration and you will hear something like, "A lack of commitment, a disconnect between what they say and how they live, complacency," or some other closely related aliment. Almost every writer on the subject of discipleship points to this as the heart of the failure of the modern church. It is non-discipleship at its very best (or worst).

Bill Hull describes this type of non-discipleship as "the elephant in the room." He wrote, "We have denied it exists; we have thrown a large table cloth over it and called it a coffee table." He goes on to say that we feed this elephant so well that it has come to dominate the church. The food that Hull says we feed it is very interesting. He said the main dish is that "everyone's commitment level is acceptable." He adds to that a side dish of "meeting the demands of the immature and the passive-aggressive underachievers." He then adds the dessert of "conflicts among those vying for power born of their pathology." And when that happens in the church, "The majority of time and effort is consumed in keeping the elephant well fed."[1]

All of these folks love to say "Lord, Lord." They are indeed the elephants in the church today. The problem is these are the very people who keep the sojourners off the road, keep others from getting on the road, and keep the leaders so busy they cannot even point to the road.

God has a sense of humor. We don't see it often in Scripture, but I see it every time I look in the mirror. I was voted the most handsome boy in high school. Today I am bald, gray, and generally find it hard to look into the mirror. (I'm glad Margaret still sees that kid of long ago.) However, every now and then we see God's sense of humor come shining through. I love the story of Mount Carmel when the 900 false prophets were trying to wake up their god. But maybe the funniest occurred in the New Testament when Paul was teaching in the hall of Tyrannus. Luke tells us that Jews and Greeks from all over Asia had come to hear him, and the number of conversions from that ministry were phenomenal. God did such extraordinary miracles through Paul, even aprons and handkerchiefs that he touched were used to heal the sick. It was so outstanding that others wanted in on the act. There were seven Jews who had been going around trying to invoke the name of Jesus and drive out demons. They would say, "In the name of Jesus, whom Paul preaches, I command you to come out" (Acts 10:13)." These men were known as the seven sons of Sceva. One day, as they were trying to perform this exorcism, an evil spirit jumped out of his victim and said to these men, "Jesus I know, and I know about Paul, but who are you?" (Acts 19:15). Then the evil spirit jumped on these men and proceeded to beat the tar out of them. Luke tells us that the spirit gave them such a beating that they ran out of the house naked and bleeding.

Every time the Lord begins to do powerful things, people line up and try to get into the act. In the 1970's and 80's television evangelism experienced extraordinary growth. Great names and great preaching grew out of that era – names like Stanley, Swindoll, Sheen, and of course Billy Graham. Television was being used of God to reach millions who would not have been reached otherwise. But following closely behind the power of God, came the deception of Satan. No sooner had television begun to grow great evangelists, Satan began to destroy as many as possible and to send in his own troops. Who can forget the names of the fallen? I am trying. And the fallen were crying "Lord, Lord."

Every generation has had such teachers.

There are many in churches all over America today who claim to be Kingdom people. They have made their confession of faith and have professed that faith at either baptism or confirmation. They appear to honor Jesus by calling Him,

"Lord," or "our Lord.'" They recite the Lord's Prayer, the Apostle's Creed, and sing hymns and praise choruses of excessive devotion to Him. And then they will get up from their pews, go out into the world, and behave as if Christ does not exist. We need to know that Jesus is not impressed by our orthodox words; He is impressed only by whether or not our hearts have led us to a radical commitment of our minds, our wills, and our lives to Him and His teaching. If not, you can call "Lord, Lord" all you want, but on that final day, you may find yourself eternally surprised when He says, "Go away from Me, I never knew you."

Don't confuse this with a gospel of works. Jesus refutes that very quickly. He said, "Many will say to Me on that day, 'Lord, Lord, did we not prophesy in Your name, and in your name drive out demons and perform many miracles?'" On the judgment day, there will be long lines of people standing in front of Jesus to be judged. In that line there will be pagans, those from other religions, blasphemers and evildoers. But there will be others in that line – people who call themselves Christian, but who have spent their lives on the broad road to destruction; there will be the false prophets who led them there; Jesus said there will even be those who confess His name as Lord, and now He adds one other group of those who think they have it made into the Kingdom, but in reality they have not. These are the miracle workers, the exorcists, and those who speak the true word of God. Yet they live their lives as if Christ never preached a sermon, died on the cross, was raised from the dead, or ascended into heaven to reign with all authority in heaven and earth.

What this means, Christian, is that you may be the Pope, your may fly around the nation making millions with Reverend attached to your name, you may be a missionary, you may be a prophet, priest, or preacher, you may be the chairman of the church elder board, or head up every committee in the church, you may have sat in one pew for so long that it is officially yours. But if you have not allowed Christ to be formed in you, don't stand in shock if the door into heaven gets slammed in your face. And the last words you hear from the Lord are, "I never knew you, you evil-doer." These are harsh and radical words – but they are not my words, they are Christ's words. He said, miracles won't get you in; speaking the truth of God will not get you in; and driving out evil spirits won't get you in – even if all that is done in His name.

There is still only one way into the Kingdom of God. Look back to verse 21, "... only he who does the will of my Father Who is in heaven." Again, those looking for contra-dictions in Scripture and theology hold this up like a banner and cry "foul." Eph.2:8 and many other passages tell us that we will never get to heaven by doing anything, that faith is the only way. But Jesus said we must do the Father's will. That clearly means works. Which is it, faith or works?

Jesus does not answer that dilemma in the Sermon on the Kingdom Road – it is not the place. The purpose of this sermon is to describe the radical transformation that will occur if we are saved. But later in His ministry, He truly brings this statement in line with faith. In John 6:40, speaking to His followers on the lakeshore He said, "For My Father's will is that everyone who looks to the Son and believes in Him shall have eternal life. I will raise Him up on that last day." See how beautifully it all holds together. The will of the Father is that we look to His Son – literally make a radical commit-ment of life and mind to Him. Then we will be saved.

John tells us in 1 John 5 that, "Everyone who believes that Jesus is the Christ is born from God... and everyone born of God overcomes the world." So we come full circle. We must be born again to be saved; we cannot be born again unless we place our trust in Jesus Christ; and the external evidence of that salvation is our overcoming the world, by obedience to God's word.

As I have studied the Sermon on the Kingdom Road over the life of my ministry, I have been greatly convicted of the intense level of obedience and discipleship demanded by Christ. He has looked me in the eye and found me wanting; the radical surrender to Kingdom principles He demands leaves me bare; but when I come to this last part I am most profoundly moved. If the road is all that narrow, am I truly walking on that road? Is my ministry consistent with the teaching of the narrow road? Because if it is not, then I am a false prophet. Week after week Jesus convicts me of my shortcomings. I liberally confess Him with my mouth. I engage in all kinds of holy work, prophesying in His name; I have even attempted deliverance ministries to free people from Satan; and yet I see now that all that is not enough. Only one thing is enough.

That one thing is echoed from the beginning to the end of the Sermon on the Kingdom Road. The only way into heaven is through Christ. He must say, "Enter, I know you," or we will not darken the gate. And when we realize how utterly impossible it is for us to meet the demands of the Sermon – to work our way in; to confess our way in; or even perform miraculous things for Him – then and only then will we recognize the utter bankruptcy of our spirits. It's at this point we land on our knees and cry out, "Lord, have mercy on me, a sinner." And to us, Jesus said, "Blessed are the bankrupt (the poor in spirit) for theirs is the kingdom of heaven." The narrow gate opens; He whispers our name and says, "Enter, I know you."

Chapter 18

Two Builders

❦

Therefore everyone who hears these words of mine and puts
them into practice is like a wise man who built his house
on the rock. The rain came down, the streams rose, and the
winds blew and beat against that house; yet it did not fall,
because it had its foundation on the rock.
But everyone who hears these words of mine and does not
put them into practice is like a foolish man who built his
house on sand. The rain came down, the streams rose, and
the winds blew and beat against that house,
and it fell with a great crash.
When Jesus had finished saying these things,
the crowds were amazed at his teaching,
because he taught as one who had authority, and not as
their teachers of the law. (Matt. 7:24-29)

One thing I have learned in my years on this earth – life is full of storms. There are the storms of courtship, the storms of marriage, the storms of child raising, the storms of careers and business, the storms of advancing age, and the storms of the unexpected events that ravage and heap destruction upon life and family. To counteract those storms,

God has blessed me with the parable of two builders. I always begin marriage and pre-marriage counseling sessions with this parable. Let me tell you an almost true story of two couples [builders] who I believe reflect the truth of this blessed teaching of our Lord.

There were two young couples who entered my study that morning.[1] Their eyes were wide; joy filled their hearts. I had known them all for a couple of years and had watched their relationships bloom and flourish. But these were not two ordinary couples. It was two brothers, who had courted and fallen in love with two sisters. They were not only blood kin; they were the best of friends. Almost everything they did, almost everywhere they went, they did and went together. So it was only natural, they wanted to get married together. And if they were going to get married together, it was only natural that they receive counseling together. It was an exciting time for them and a very unique experience for me.

I began my counseling the same way I begin all marriage counseling sessions. I tell of God's plan for marriage and how a successful marriage is built upon a solid foundation of His word. It's like the two builders in Jesus' parable at the conclusion of the Sermon on the Kingdom Road. One built upon a solid foundation (hearing God's word and putting it into practice) and the other upon a foundation of sand (hearing God's word and ignoring it). And when the storms came, one withstood the storm and the other did not. Marriage is like that. We can build upon God's word, His precepts, and His commands; and while this will not prevent the storms from coming, it will give us the power to withstand them. So we can build our marriages to withstand the storms or we can choose to ignore God's word and go our own ways.

So the counseling began. Both couples listened carefully to my words that first morning. David and Laurie were more attentive than Dan and Lucy, and as time went by, the gap between their attentiveness seemed to widen. David and Laurie seemed mesmerized by God's magnificent plan for marriage. They took notes, asked questions, and made commitments to each other along the way. But Dan and Lucy, they were a different story. They seemed far more romantic than David and Laurie. They couldn't keep their hands off each other. The outward displays of affection were distracting and, in my mind, inappropriate.

The sessions continued for several weeks as the time of the wedding was rapidly approaching. Both girls launched themselves into the wedding preparations. It was going to be as lavish as it was unique. There was a bubbly, joyous agreement on the colors, the ceremony, and the arrangements. The boys, on the other hand, seemed confused by all the hubbub, but willingly went along. They were both experiencing a dream come true, and they were not about to mess it up by offering advice. And I was convinced that although their marriages would be very different, they would be filled with the blessings of God. The day came on a wonderful June, Saturday evening. And as the depth of preparation would dictate, the ceremony went off without a hitch. The town could not remember such a wedding and reception. And off the beautiful couples went to a week-long honeymoon.

They got back to town on the following Saturday evening. David and Laurie missed church that first Sunday home, but the following Tuesday morning, they were in my office full of excitement. While on their honeymoon in Kauai, they visited a church there that was dear to my own heart. They were anxious to share with me the pastor's message. They told me he spoke on the Sermon on the Kingdom Road. It was as if God was confirming to them everything we had discussed in counseling.

I asked if Dan and Lucy had made the worship service, and they replied, "No! You know how those two love birds are. We couldn't rouse them from their rooms." We all laughed, but secretly, there was a check in my spirit – something that I stored for a later day.

The next several years, it was exciting to watch David and Laurie grow in the Lord. Shortly after they returned from their honeymoon, they became active leaders in the youth group. After only a couple of years, it was evident that David was elder material. So the church board invited him to become a deacon for the next four years as a training ground for the deeper spiritual journey as an elder. Laurie was also devoted to service in the church. Whenever someone was sick or emotionally hurting, Laurie was there with a prayer and a meal. She attended every available Bible study, and it was clear before long, she was fully qualified to teach some of our small group studies. It was exciting to watch these two surrendered lives grow in their relationship with the Lord.

A sad thing happened to David and Laurie after only three years of marriage. Laurie learned she was pregnant, and I do not remember seeing any couple quite so excited about bringing a new life into the world. The whole church entered into the celebration with them. Showers were given, the nursery was prepared, and all necessities for the new life were in place. Then one morning, about eight and one-half months into the pregnancy, Laurie could not feel the baby move. She called for prayer and then drove off to the doctor in the nearby city. A sono-gram confirmed her deepest fear. Little Joe was dead – the umbilical cord was wrapped around his neck.

I will never forget the funeral. The entire church and much of the rest of the community was standing at the graveside. Then, at the end of the message, David stood in front of the entire crowd. He said, "Pastor, may I say a word?" and without waiting for my response, "I just need everyone to know, that there is no way that Laurie and I could get through this, if Jesus Christ were not at our side." And then without fanfare, he sat down, leaving not one dry eye in the cemetery.

A couple of years later, Laurie was accused of taking money from her company till. It was late one evening when the police knocked on their door. Laurie, already dressed for bed, answered the knock, and with the most profound apology, the officer arrested her. She was humiliated beyond belief. Here she was, a leader in the church, well respected in the community, and a faithful teacher of the church youth – sitting in the county jail. The incident came about when the owner of the company told Laurie, that he would make the deposit on the way home. But before he got to the bank, he stopped at the local bar – as he did on more than one occasion. He became intoxicated that night and in his stupor, he forgot about the money. The next day, Laurie opened the store as usual. When the owner came in he asked about deposit of the night before. She reminded him that he made the deposit. Not another word was spoken, but by nightfall, the owner called the police, accusing Laurie of the theft. Two days later, the owner of the company found the money under the front seat of his car. Embarrassed, he told the police and the charges against Laurie were dropped.

Having heard the news, a lawyer was camped on David and Laurie's doorstep by that evening. He urged the couple to sue the business owner. He chuckled, "By next week, you can own that business." The couple politely dismissed the attorney and immediately went to the company owner and prayed with the employer. The next day Laurie returned to her old job and never another word was spoken of the event.

Over the last ten years, David and Laurie had their fair share of set-backs — lay-offs for David, financial hard times, illnesses and other events that pound against life and marriage. Yet through it all, they rebounded and became stronger and stronger in their love for each other and in the power of their faith.

Dan and Lucy were quite another story. I didn't see much of them after the wedding. They came to church a few times that first year, but after that they became part of the C& E (Christmas and Easter) Club. Between Dan's golf and Lucy's tennis, their fellowship with Christ grew very dim. From all outward appearances, they seemed to be the happy couple. They built a beautiful home in the country. Dan had a wonderful job and had even been written up in a state newspaper as a rising young star in the business world. After about five years of marriage, they began their family. They had a boy and a girl, two years apart. They were the apple of the social community's eyes. No social event was complete without this couple in attendance.

Dan's golf became an obsession. He began to gamble heavily on the golf course. Soon the gambling debts began to pile up. They re-mortgaged their home, but before long it was apparent, they must sell it. Yet, he kept on gambling – waiting for that big win to bail him out. Eventually, he had to declare bankruptcy, in order to save what little they had left. During all this, it was rumored that Lucy was having an affair with her tennis instructor. In fact, I think Dan was the only one in town who didn't know it – or at least he didn't care.

On one occasion, they called me for marriage counseling. After listening to their story, I reminded them of our pre-marriage study, but they did not want to hear about it. I asked them to examine the joy in David and Laurie's life, but Dan quickly said, "David's a nerd. He has become a religious fanatic. He never has any real fun." He said, "You know, David used to be a 2 handicapper on the golf course, but now he hardly ever plays. He always has to do something with Laurie. I tell you, that woman is smothering him."

By the end of that session, Lucy was in tears. Daniel had lost all interest in her. Golf was his passion, and he paid more attention to *Playboy* magazine than to her. At one point, she begged Dan to listen to what he was saying. But his heart was stone cold. After that day, I never saw the couple again. They divorced a few months later. Lucy and her children moved to another community. Custody battles ensued. And this once loving couple, who could not keep their hands off each other, felt nothing but hatred.

You see, both couples heard the words of Jesus Christ. David and Laurie, while they were not perfect, lived their lives by their best understanding of those words. Dan and Lucy on the other hand, heard those same words, but believed they were just words from a preacher and meant nothing to their lives. Storms came to both lives. It was like they were standing in front of a hurricane. The winds of life beat and blew against both families. David and Laurie had built their marriage on the teaching of Jesus, and no matter the ferocity of the storm, their marriage grew stronger. But Dan and Lucy just could not believe that the words of 2000 years ago had any relevance to the modern American marriage. And when the storms of life came their way, the marriage fell with a great crash.

There is truth in Jesus' words. Or maybe I should say, Jesus' words are truth. That means that every word uttered from His mouth has ultimate significance. It is when we surrender to this fact that Christ can begin to be formed in us. He captures our attention with words that become a mirror for us to look deeply into. And when we look into that mirror we don't like the reflection. It drives us to our knees in utter poverty of spirit. That is the beginning of the Road, the journey that leads to life eternal. My mirror is not quite as foggy as it was twenty years ago, but I am certain, it will be even clearer tomorrow and the next day as I continue my journey. I keep collecting bugs on my windshield along the way, so daily cleaning is a necessity. But as I think of the alternative way, a journey which may seem right at the time, I see the broken lives of Dan and Lucy, the shattered dreams of substance abuse, the ruttiness of the rut, or the dullness of a mirror not yet clear, and I find that my desire to keep my windshield clean drives me morning by morning into my study with my King.

Epilogue

꧁꧂

"When Jesus had finished saying these things, the crowds were amazed at His teaching, because He taught as One who had authority, and not as their teachers of the law."
(Matt. 7:28-29)

An elderly man walked into the doctor's office. He was clean and, well dressed, even though it was obvious he was poor. He sat quietly in the waiting room, patiently awaiting his turn. When the nurse came out to escort him back to the examination room, words of "ma'am" and "thank you" came from his lips. When the doctor entered the room, the old man rose, extended his hand, and greeted the professional with, "Good morning Dr. Jones."

Another man entered the waiting room. He was young, unkempt, and disrespectful of the office staff. He demanded attention and when the doctor finally saw him, the greeting was, "Hey man, service is sure slow around here. My time has value too." What is missing in the second patient is something that is sorely missing in our culture today. It is respect for authority.

I notice it in my own ministry. The older generation cannot bring themselves to call me Bud. It's always "Reverend," "Pastor," or "Dr." But never "Bud." But Dr. or Mrs. or Mr.

or Reverend or Madam or even Your Majesty, are superficial titles we banter around between us human folks. In the end, in the eyes of God we are all the same. However, there is an authority that is indisputable. It is not one bestowed externally. It cannot be altered or tarnished. It is the authority that comes from deep within the heart of God. Only One Man in all of human history walked with this authority.

When Jesus had finished delivering the Sermon, the crowds were amazed at His teaching. He had delivered the greatest message ever preached with such great authority. So I must ponder, when these words are spoken from the One who has authority, how do we deal with the upside down concepts of the Kingdom? How do we cope with poverty of spirit, heart forgiveness, plucking out eyes and detaching members? How do we keep from worrying or fighting the battles with weapons of love? How do we keep from lusting or getting angry? These things are so difficult that some try to water down the teaching. They say the Sermon was delivered at the beginning of Jesus' ministry. Therefore, it was before grace and the cross. It was before Pentecost and the coming of the Holy Spirit. Yes, it was all those things. But notice that Jesus taught of eternal matters. Eternal matters extend beyond the cross, the resurrection, Pentecost, the Protestant Reformation, and televangelism. Jesus taught people of every generation how to live the only way that gives the abundant life that He so desperately wants us to experience. Jesus wants His hearers to become His disciples, not to boost His ego, but to give us the very meaning and purpose for which He created us. The Kingdom Road is not an easy one to walk on, but it is the only road that contains joy for our souls. And Jesus gave it to us with such authority.

Endnotes

Introduction
[1] A. W. Tozer, *The Attributes of God, Volume One, A Journey Into the Father's Heart*, (Camp Hill: Christian Publications, Inc. 1997), 3.

Chapter 1
[1] John R.W. Stott, *The Message of the Sermon on the Mount, The Bible Speaks Today*, (Inter-Varsity Press: Leicester; Downers Grove, 1978), 19.

Chapter 2
[1] Richard Bach, *Jonathan Livingston Seagull: a story*, (The McMillan Company: New York, 1970), 55.

Chapter 3
[1] Arthur W. Pink, *An Exposition of the Sermon on the Mount*, Tenth Printing, (Baker Book House: Grand Rapids, 1950, 1953), 29.

Chapter 4
[1] Stott, 91.

Chapter 5
[1] In 1969, Stanley Rosenblatt wrote a book called *Divine Rocket*. In his well intentioned book, he tried to come to an understanding of why the divorce rate in America had risen from one in seven prior to the Great War to one in four in the 1960's. From his analysis, he offered a solution, which we now call "no fault divorce." The State of California was the first to adopt his theory and by the end of 1969, they passed no-fault divorce legislation. Within five years, 45 states followed suit and by

1985 every state had no fault divorce laws on its books. In stark contrast to Rosenblatt's theory, no-fault divorce caused a skyrocketing escalation of divorce. Over the next 10 years, the divorce rate in America grew by 250 percent and by 1995, one out of every two first time marriages ended in divorce and 70 percent of all subsequent marriages fell on the altar of divorce.

[2] Aunt Tad and Harl O'Brien built a church in Kenya; she was head of the prayer chain of her church; and her generosity helped me in the early stages of my ministry. There are not enough pages to tell all they did for the Kingdom of God.

Chapter 6
[1] I know there are many who cannot relate to their fathers in a positive way. But please read on, because you do have a Father who is more than you could ever ask or imagine. Ask my wife. She can relate.

Chapter 9
[1] John Piper, *Don't Waste Your Life,*(Crossways: Wheaton, 2003) *p. 99*

Chapter 10
[1] How Bundy's became addicted to pornography is speculation on my part. However, the reality of his addiction is historical fact.

Chapter 13
[1] Oswald Chambers, *My Utmost for His Highest,* Undated Edition, (Discovery House Publishers: Grand Rapids, 1992), Jan. 1.

Chapter 14
[1] Stott, 190.

Chapter 16
[1] Dietrich Bonhoeffer, *Cost of Discipleship,*(New York: Simon and Schuster, 1959), 45.

Chapter 17
[1] Bill Hull, *Choose the Life, Exploring a Faith That Embraces Discipleship,* (Baker Books: Grand Rapids, 2004), 71.

Chapter 18

[1] In actuality, these two couples, while their stories are true, do not exist. They are a compilation of my counseling experience, both pre-marriage and post marriage.